Graciella la Gitana
Oracle Deck
Companion Book

Theresa Varela PhD

New York

Pollen Press Publishing, LLC
New York

First Edition

Copyright © 2025 by Theresa Varela

All rights reserved. No part of this book may be used or reproduced in any manner whatsoever without written permission except in the case of brief quotations embodied in critical articles or reviews.

Theresa Varela
theresa@theresavarela.com
www.theresavarela.com

Book Cover and Interior Designed by Patricia Dornelles
Production by Patricia Dornelles
Distributed by IngramSpark

Library of Congress Control Number: 2025914101
Names: Varela, Theresa, author
        Cordova, Mara Alicia, illustrator
        Dornelles, Patricia, editor

Title: Graciella la Gitana: Oracle Deck Companion Handbook
Description: New York, Pollen Press Publishing [2025]
Identifiers: Paperback ISBN: 978-1-7327167-8-0
Subjects: 1. Self-help. 2.Spirituality 3. Oracle

Works by Theresa Varela

Novels

Covering the Sun with My Hand

Coney Island Siren

Daisy Muñiz Mystery Series:

Nights of Indigo Blue

Murder in Red Hook

Poetry

Answered by Silence: A Collection of Poems

Oracle

Graciella la Gitana Oracle

El Oráculo de Graciella la Gitana

Dedication

To all those who seek clarity and to Graciella, who always responds with wisdom, love, and profound compassion.

Table of Contents

Introduction..1

The Cards

Ancestors / Ancestros..12
Autumn / Otoño..15
Bravado / Bravata...18
Cape / Capa..21
Celebration / Celebración..24
Change / Cambios...26
Contemplation / Contemplación..28
Cosmos / Cosmos..31
Dance / Baile..33
Darkness / Oscuridad..36
Death / Muerte...38
Earth / Tierra...40
East / Este...42
Fear / Temor..44
Fertility / Fertilidad..46
Fidelity / Fidelidad...48
Fire / Fuego...50
Fool / Tonto...52
Fortune Teller / Adivinadora...55
Friendship / Amistad..58
Gatherer / Recolectora...60
Gypsy / Gitana...62
Health / Salud..64
Impasse / Punto Muerto...66
Intimacy / Intimidad...68
Kindness / Caridad...70
Lament / Llanto..72
Madam / Madama...74
Moon / Luna...76

North / Norte	78
Opportunity / Oportunidad	80
Patience / Paciencia	82
Position / Posición	84
Poverty / Pobreza	86
Prisoner / Prisionera	88
Rascal / El Travieso	90
Romantic / Romántica	92
Sobriety / Sobriedad	94
South / Sur	96
Spiral / Espiral	99
Spring / Primavera	101
Star / Estrella	103
Summer / Verano	105
Sun / Sol	107
Temptation / Tentación	109
Temptress / Sirena	111
Toreador / Matador	113
Traveler / Viajera	115
Treachery / Traición	117
Wagon / Carreta	119
Water / Agua	121
West / Oeste	123
Wind / Viento	125
Winter / Invierno	127
Wisdom / Sabiduría	129
Writer / Escritora	131
Spreads	**133**
Sample layout designs	**135**

Introduction

The Graciella la Gitana Oracle© was whispered to me by my spirit guide, Graciella la Gitana (pronounced hē-tah-nah), over twenty years ago. It was created slowly and tenderly by me and the illustrator, my daughter, Mara Alicia Cordova. It is through Graciella's pictorial narrative that she wishes to help us delve deep within ourselves and garner the gifts of stillness that may afford us peace of mind and sanity of spirit.

When I initially began working on this oracle, I believed it was to be a tarot deck. I began designing it as such, but the project had more ebbs than flows. I was advised by a spiritualist who I respect greatly that the deck is an oracle, and once I had this information, the work truly began to move forward. Sitting in meditation with Graciella, words, concepts, and inklings of what the illustrations for this oracle would be were revealed. I shared the images I received with Mara, who created them initially in blue-penciled thumbnails and then acrylics. The digital medium she ultimately chose manifested the cards in depth, coloration, and expression that we both believe are most loyal to this oracle. Graciella gleefully agreed. The resulting oracle is dynamic and alive, pragmatic yet magical.

The original table of contents in the booklet that accompanies the oracle deck is presented in sections that are depicted in the way that Graciella requested it be shown. When we have learned to use the oracle, we become familiar with sequences that are important to Graciella and, ultimately, her story.

The layout of the table of contents is significant for Graciella. As directed, I began the table of contents with the four directions- east, south, west, and north that are presented with a foundation in the spiritual based traditions taught to me by my elder Oh Shinnah Fastwolf known for her tireless teachings on loving and living on our Mother Earth. The east is a place for illumination, the light within ourselves that extends to our environments, the south is the domain of trust and innocence, the west is the realm of introspection and our personal spiritual paths, and the north is the home of our ancestors and those who have crossed over.

We then move toward the elements known to be air, water, earth, and fire. Air is symbolic of the intellect, water the emotions, earth our sensations, and fire represents our intuitions. The seasons-winter, spring, summer, and fall and all the transformative states are presented next. Finally, Graciella's life. We start with her young years, move through her challenging years, her flow of love and salvation with kindness toward others and herself, and lastly, the enrichment of Graciella's life through connections with family, ancestors, and other relationships. Her life on this planet is very much like ours.

Life events are not linear and can be seen as spirals. While we believe we may be going through similar events repeatedly, we are facing them at different levels and intensities. We experience them with our knowledge, from prior encounters or even parallel worlds and are better able to achieve fulfillment and gratification in our existences. Graciella asks that we not become wedded to linear events in our lives. By being open to fluidity and shifting images and concepts we experience a more profound depth to our beings.

For ease, we have chosen to produce this volume with an alphabetized table of contents.

The Oracle

Consulting an oracle for esoteric knowledge is a spiritual practice that began in the earliest of times. An oracle is an instrument for divination, just as bones, tarot, shells, feathers, palms, tea leaves, and ice offer wisdom in advice. A seer has a vast array of tools for divination. Culture and tradition, along with personal resonance, often dictate which instrument is chosen by the querent.

By seeking the oracle, a quest is begun for advice, suggestion, revelation of veiled information, or affirmation or refutation of that which the querent believes they know. The new seeker is often unaware of the pandimensional nature of information that comes from an oracle, but by steadily committing to work with it becomes conscious that they themselves are an integral strand of the web of knowledge offered by the oracle.

This oracle is comprised of concepts that we commonly face in the mundane world that we are charged to experience in an extraordinary way. When consulting with this oracle, the seeker is engaging with Graciella's energy, which manifests through the cards. One of her desires is to encourage those who undertake quests for knowledge to create relationships with their own spirits and spiritual guides in both visible and invisible form.

Graciella la Gitana

My bond with Graciella developed during a time when I began to embrace my spirituality and practice as a Spiritualist. In addition to attending women's Goddess ceremonies, sacred fires, sweat lodges, and *misas*, spiritual séances, I've sat in many hours of meditation and learned to listen to Spirit. I've been fortunate to have had mentors from different traditions guide me in pristine spiritual practices of light. Graciella came forth and began to share her vision with me. Graciella's name is synonymous with grace and wit, a characteristic that is translated in Spanish as *graciosa*, gracious, and graceful. She is of Spanish, Moorish, and Romany heritages, and during her time on Earth, in the early 1900s, traveled through Spain, Africa, Egypt, and the Moorish territories extensively. She sparkles, and her presence brings forth a sensual connection to life; her service is one of compassion and charitable works. Graciella loves to dance and stoke the fires of life!

Graciella tells us that her lifetime in the spiritual realm is most satisfying, and she has hopes that the day will come when more people on this plane unite with their spiritual guides and partake of the abundant spiritual support that is available to all. Exploring and deepening relationships with one's own spirit guides can provide love, intimate connections, guidance, and protection in all aspects of our lives. Graciella is timeless. When I access her presence through meditation, she opens the door to her abode. The sensual aromas of cooking permeate the air that I breathe, the colors, textures, and fabrics of her furnishings are tantalizing. Graciella is of beauty and loves beauty. She offers comfort, healing, a place to sit and enjoy tranquility, and fulfillment of the soul.

Graciella encourages you to feel the beauty within you and your life experiences. Remember to approach these cards with love while exploring the various aspects of your personal story through Graciella's narrative. The challenges which bring us to approach oracle consultations build strength in all facets of ourselves. Connecting with our spiritual natures and our spiritual guides help us to manage the tumultuous events of the world in relation to our beings.

Take time to close your eyes and feel Graciella's presence. Indeed, she is with you. Graciella declares, *This is my memoir. This is my story, and compasión is the element I have consistently been shown is necessary for our collective good and growth throughout eternity.*

We tend to think of the elements as earth, water, fire, and air. The element of compassion is one that is fundamental in the survival of not only our personal existences but in the healthy thriving of the world in which we live. Compassion for self and others is essential for humans to fulfill their destinies and to provide the support and love for others who need succor as we energetically dance our exchanges in this Universe. We are so much more than we know ourselves to be. We take turns in giving and receiving.

The element of compassion is not as complicated to work with as one may believe. A simple recipe for a dish of compassion asks for a sprinkle of love and a dash of sympathy. There are people who mistake compassion for pity. They take offense when they feel the energy of compassion coming toward them. They say, *I don't need pity!* It may be difficult for them to believe that others may want to help, to love, to provide sustenance because we are fellows, not because we believe we are better than another. Gardeners use compassion while tending to a bed of soil. There is some toiling, but there is also a joy in digging one's fingers in the earth to prepare a rich source for growth. Graciella speaks of many instances in her life where an act of compassion has literally saved her from walking down a path toward ruination. The person who reached out a hand to aide in her alighting from a coach, who shared a plump red tomato when she was in the depths of hunger, and those who chose to give her an opportunity to work for wages despite a crime that she committed were all working with the element of compassion. Graciella speaks of being indebted to the kind hearts who touched hers.

The element of compassion is given to us for our use and is plentifully supplied by our Universe. How an individual chooses to work with this element is their choice. There are those who ignore the growth of trees. Yes, they may admire the splendid colors of the leaves in *otoño*, autumn, but what other regard have they afforded the individual tree or the forest? There is the person who walks enjoying the grounds of his estate and the swath of trees that are lush, green, and flourish. But what is he thinking of as he walks? He may be thinking of building a new construct of offices and with that comes the pouring of concrete and building systems that would halt the flow of the river and affect its livestock. He is thinking about deforestation, but he is not aware of it as he ambles through his well-tended gardens.

Take a moment here to meditate on the concept of compassion. Light a candle. Nestle into a comfortable position sitting, kneeling, or lying down. Whichever is the most comfortable for you. Close your eyes. Let your thoughts wander. Allow sensations and feelings to flow without predetermination. Observe, as acts of compassion float in and out of your consciousness. These may be acts committed by others or you. They may have been done for others or for you. Become aware of how compassion has already filled your life.

When you feel ready, open your eyes, and take your pen and fill a few pages with passages of your reignited knowledge of compassion. Fill yourself with this knowledge. Experience them in your dreams tonight. You are an element of compassion.

Meditation

Meditation is a practice that is as essential as drinking water and nourishing oneself with food. For me, meditation usually consists of sitting during the in-between times after smudging with sage burned in my beloved abalone shell, centering, and being transported to deep connection and communication with Graciella. After each session, I write down that which I hear. You too will have access to her when questing this oracle. We encourage you to use the practices of meditation and centering that resonate most with you.

Think of meditation as a check-in time for yourself, by yourself, with yourself. Have you noticed any external obstacles that you may have put in place that are mere tools you've used that represent internal resistance? The following are statements you may have made that reflect that resistance.

-I don't have time.

-I will leave myself too open.

-I'm afraid.

-I can't concentrate.

-What is it good for?

-I still don't have time

But yes, you do have time to sit with yourself and get to know your inner mechanisms, like the workings of a clock. A clock may tell time but does not tell you what to do with your time. It is up to you. You have free will. Ah! Free will may be the key. Are you willing to get to know yourself or are you too fearful? You, of course, may be horrified at the prospect of looking within but then again, you may be surprised and filled with joy at what you may find.

The willingness to go in takes effort and you are worth it.

Pronoun disclaimer

Our writings broadly use the pronoun *she* for ease and this is Graciella's oracle. Together, all of us who have worked with Graciella for the creation, design, and translation of her work live with the knowledge that masculine and feminine traits are fluid in all gender expressions. Everyone determines what that expression signifies for them and how it will manifest for them.

Drawing oracle cards

Each morning, I smudge, center, shuffle the deck, fan the cards on a firm surface, and pull a card. On a hectic day, I just close my eyes and draw a card. The concept of the card provides me with a sense of what I will be facing during the day. The oracle provides guidance as to how I might deal with an issue, problem, or situation. I usually place the card aside and revisit it again at night for a brief reflection of what I encountered during the day, the manifestation of my earlier visualization. I am often in awe at how the card has mirrored my day's experiences. When engaged in readings for others, I am always rewarded with new insights on each concept that pertains directly to the person who sits in front of me.

The text that is offered along with the illustrations are suggestions about the meanings of each individual card. When gazing at the illustrations, be aware of color, form, symbolism, and texture. I continue to find new meanings each time I consult the cards. Although they are in a seemingly static form, they are living and breathing. Allow yourself to dance with the vibration of each.

Graciella and I believe that you might best enjoy these cards playfully. Consult the back of this oracle companion book for suggested layout designs. You may ultimately create your own spreads or layout designs that resonate with you once you have developed a relationship with the oracle. Mostly, use this oracle simply and with love.

Building relationship with the cards

Sit with the cards. Take them to work with you or to the park. Show them around your world. Smudge them with sage or cigar smoke. Place them on your altar. Infuse them with the power of your spirit. Light a white candle at night and allow the cards to bask in the glory of calm and stillness. Take caution not to leave the candles unattended. Your safety is primary.

The objective is to invite your cards to know you and you to know your cards. Allow them to become one with you. Breathe on them. Shuffle them. Hold them to your chest, your heartspace. Become friends with them.

As you become familiar with the images, you will become more acquainted with your style of reading cards. Readers from different backgrounds and experiences will attribute varying meanings to items in the cards. For example, in the poverty card, the guitar in the window of the pawn shop may signify the loss of music or art in one's life, the gem might portray the richness that one is missing in their life, the gold charm bracelet that Graciella holds in her hand may mean the release of friendship or the desire to keep a meaningful friendship despite the hardship endured. The cards may take on different meanings over time. With practice you will experience new symbolic meanings in the images.

While the passages below each picture may be a guide for a new reader, each reader is encouraged to also see with their inner eye. You will bring your own experience to the words that you share with the person who sits in front of you. Allow your intuition to speak during the reading. Over time, you will see how easy that becomes. Don't think too hard or too long. Allow what comes to come. Stay positive. Change is often scary for many people. Try not to allow your pragmatism to overtake your imagination. Be supportive in your delivery. Allow yourself to see with all your senses. Remember that you are the embodiment of compassion.

Ancestors / Ancestros

What is invisible can be felt with your soul
Open your heart and let your faith ignite
We are with you all the days of your life
You are never alone

Graciella prays over a sacred fire. She holds her hands above the heat of the flame, allowing her energy to be at one with the fire. The ancestors are in her presence, ever engaged. She is in prayer and conversing with her spirit guides.

We tend to think of our ancestors as those who lived before us in our familial lineage, however, the ancestors that communicate with us may be outside of our blood line. The ancestor may be someone or a being who has lived similarly to us and can share their acquired knowledge. They may be of different cultures, ethnicities, and races which are earthly distinctions. They may be in animal or plant form. Be open to their manifestation in your life. These spirit guides share the eye-opening bliss of love, of progression in our lives, and of engaging in works of compassion. They may help us to access gifts deep within us that may be outside of our awareness. These guides have chosen to work with us of their own free will and because you are ready.

There are lessons to learn during our lifetimes. Ancestral communication comes in many forms. Visualizations, words, and scents are some of the most common signs that the ancestors are conversing with us. We are free to choose to accept the wisdom of the spiritual beings that come to us and challenge us to go beyond the boundaries to which we are accustomed. Our ancestors are always with us extending support and guidance. It is paramount to discern who we will allow to work with us. We are advised to always request that the energy be of the purest light and of the highest good for us.

Some of us engage with ancestors who are relatives that we were close to before they crossed over, such as a grandmother or a sibling. We may miss the presence of some of these beings in the physical form, but it is important to know that relationships continue even after seeming death. There are some ancestors who come to us sparingly. We may have recurring dreams that we recognize as foretelling our immediate futures.

Some individuals say that the relationships they had with family members while still alive were toxic and that there can never be healing of old wounds. Graciella tells us that there is always an opportunity for healing. As we read in the Bhagavad Gita, *Never the spirit was born, the spirit shall cease to be never.* Remember that communications, processing, and growth do not stop. We are spirits in a material form always growing and changing in our openness if we allow ourselves to do so. Prayer, meditation, and reflection can help to elucidate our relationships with our ancestors. These actions will expand and deepen wonderfully strong connections with loved ones, old and new, who come to bestow their wisdom upon us toward transformation.

Reflection: Today, I will reflect on the ancestors who have revealed themselves to me. I sit in contemplation. Is it for my highest good to allow them to share the gifts that they are so readily and eager to share? Am I ready for what they may reveal?

Affirmation: I am open to connecting to the highest good and wisdom of my ancestors.

Autumn / Otoño

Leaves swiftly fall from tree branches
Release what no longer thrives
Without bitterness but with gratitude
A tingle of sentiment flows through your being

The image shows leaves of red, orange, and gold against a sky of azure blue in their journey as they float to the accepting ground.

The incarnations of life eventually decay and dissipate. But even as the leaves seem to lose their lives, they offer protection to the earth, the bugs, plants, shrubbery, the trees, and all lifeforms that are vulnerable to the elements. Splendiferous gardens grow abundantly because of these protective coverings.

Graciella tells us that it is time to consider letting go of that which no longer serves us and prepare for the thriving life that is hidden behind that which we may not wish to release. We may be holding onto uncomfortable feelings or resentments, and the bitterness of the heart that accompanies them. The energy that goes into keeping the fires of negativity roaring is detrimental to the growth and openness that we seek on our life paths. It may be far easier to swallow our feelings and to pretend that we don't have them. We may even secretly enjoy the spark of anger that remains instilled in us as we choose not to forgive.

The action of release may entail moving from a home or a job that is no longer fruitful for us. We are advised to free ourselves of the clutter and chaos in our lives that has gathered with or without our awareness. Change is a welcome concept as it is an essential part of life. Many of us are unable to move on with a positive outlook. Do we believe that if our home or job was joyous at a point in our lives and we are in gratitude that we should continue to live or serve there? Think deeply. Reflect on your past assessment of the situation. We grow and change. Our outside circumstances are often mirror images of our inner transformations, but we need to look to see.

There are many measures to choose from, dependent on the expansiveness or depth of the situation, that will aid in releasing what no longer serves us. Writing letters to people we may have harmed or who we believe have harmed us and then burning them is a long-time strategy. Some of us bury these letters deep in the sand, while others drown them in a lake of love. Speaking aloud of our emotional wounds to another may afford us a profound sense of relief. We ask someone we trust to hear our words. Close your eyes and determine which path of release is most healthy for you.

Seal the ending of the ritual of release you have chosen in prayer for yourself and the individual or situation you have held without recourse for too long. After completing the release, allow yourself empty space and quiet time for your healing. Allow yourself to truly heal before embracing something new and worthy of you into that space.

Reflection: As I willingly release, I give thanks for its presence in my life. It has served its purpose and I am in gratitude.

Affirmation: *I release that which no longer serves me for my higher good.*

Bravado / Bravata

*Confront or retreat
There is no shame in either
Be sure your heart can withstand your maneuver
Whichever you choose, do so with dignity*

Graciella stands at the base of a tree in a small pond in the dark of night. She is covered in a dress, head scarf, and shawl of deep purples. With one hand Graciella holds her skirt away from the water and with the other hand, she holds a knife. Her countenance is one of determination. She is protected by a grove of trees. We assume that she is about to cut down a bundle that hangs from a branch. Or it may very well be that she has just placed that bundle on the tree limb.

Working toward a goal may seem ruthless. Sometimes self-care is seen as selfish. Bravado can be necessary when our bundles of treasures, goals, and dreams are in places that may be difficult to reach. Others may think or make negative statements about our drive or what seems to be relentless pursuit to advance ourselves. Those opinions do not belong to us. When we decide to act, it is of utmost importance that we are able to stand behind it. It may be distracting or feel harmful to our self-esteem when others don't believe in us. It is essential for our growth and development to continue having trust and faith in ourselves and our Higher Powers when we take an action for the good of ourselves or for others.

The Bravado card reminds us that it takes courage to move into a spot we covet. The word covet has a negative connotation in that for centuries it has been taken to mean desiring what belongs to another. The idea that to covet means having an inordinate desire for something without it belonging to someone else may take some time to understand and assimilate. If we are not ready to move forward and need more time for our dreams to come to fruition, it is perfectly reasonable to keep our desires and dreams out of reach to others who may swoop in with an attempt to remove them from us.

Important is the knowledge that there is enough, more than enough, in the abundant Universes for us all to prosper. Reach out for the treasure you covet. Only you know your true motives and your aims. If you can show up to defend yourself with clear consciousness, do so. There is enough room and prosperity in the Universe for all of us.

Reflection: What are my true motives and aims? Can I foresee any damage that may incur as a result of the decision I make? Am I seeing through my own vision for myself or through my fears of others' opinions? Am I doing this for the greater good of myself or the whole?

Affirmation: *I stand up for the good of myself and others and will do so with dignity.*

Cape / La Capa

A garment used to tease, hide, and protect
Maneuvered like a second skin swirling in the air
Planned execution of thought with action yields results
You are ready for the match

The toreador swings their red cape flamboyantly as they prepare to act. Their movements are stealth and grand and, yet they stand facing a brick wall.

Graciella tells us that while the cape may be used to taunt and tease, it can also provide protection, warmth, a place for one to hide, and for some individuals to manifest magic. The cape is meant to be a protective mantle. It distracts, it angers, and can be used to outmaneuver outside forces we would like to keep at bay or under our control.

Know that everyone is vulnerable. Also know that all have access to security. The cloak allows us to hide our motives and to cover what we don't want others to see. There is a certain arrogance to flinging our capes over our shoulders and declaring we are invulnerable to the hurts, pains, and abject sorrows that may be hurled at us. Or we use our cloaks to frighten individuals with our mannerisms. We also tease and bully others when engaging in these ploys.

When we perceive that we are merely protecting ourselves, our medicines, or our ideas from others, we may also be keeping ourselves at bay from our own true natures. We keep ourselves away from our very own circles of love. Imagine yourself confined behind a big red wall. Nothing comes in and nothing goes out. While occasionally this may be a wise visualization, done too often it can become an unintended prison. Some of us use our anger as a barrier that doesn't allow anyone to either enter or to leave our lives. We are at a standstill. Instead of allowing fear to get the better of you, allow the wall to dissipate and experience what transpires.

The motivation may be here, and you are primed to take action. But you may find that you are facing a brick wall. Life is occasionally like that. We may believe that we are ready for the fight, the dance, the move, but the support or the mechanisms we need haven't yet been constructed. Rather than continue to take action that is unrewarding or frustrating in your inability to make progress, consider what other actions you may take. Retreating can be an action. Waiting for timing to be right is another. There is nothing wrong with holding off what you may erroneously believe needs to get done immediately. Why not consider temporarily participating in another activity? Use your garnered strength where it will be most effective.

Reflection: Instead of making bold dramatic moves that lead nowhere, what actions would be most beneficial to me at this time?

Affirmation: *I measure my actions and allow patience and the desire for manifestation to harmonize.*

Celebration / Celebración

Generations gather and rejoice
Celebrate in gratitude
Enjoy the spirit of life
Share beyond the physical world

A family of several generations comes together at twilight in music to celebrate. They are deep within the woods and surround a sacred fire.

We are each gifted in unique ways on this earth, and we are encouraged to acknowledge the goodness in our lives. We are urged to make time for celebration. Birthdays, weddings, christenings, and initiations are events that we generally salute, but there are other times deserving of recognition that we may not think to honor. Graciella encourages us to celebrate those things that we are proud of. They may be relationships, creative works, or may even be the decluttering of a closet overflowing with what is no longer needed in our life.

Celebrating the lives of our friends and families may take extra energy or added steps from the patterns we usually adhere to but the resulting joy that emanates from our loved ones makes it all worth it.

We respect them with festivities or a card or a gift to show them our appreciation. We may be the ones to remind them that they are valued and worthy of recognition. When we champion the triumphs of someone other than ourselves it becomes a celebration.

Take some time out today to celebrate the accomplishments in your life. A happy family? Go for it. A realization that a project needs more work? That too! There is no reason to trudge and drudge through your daily life without taking time to breathe in nature's scents, sing the songs of happiness, and dance the steps of the Divine. All too often we work, toil, sweat, and begin the process all over again without taking time to celebrate what has been completed or what is in motion.

Reflection: What areas in my life are cause for celebration? Do I acknowledge my progress in a situation that has called for perseverance? What can I do to embrace the good things in my life?

Affirmation: *I honor myself and my loved ones and celebrate all that has been accomplished thus far.*

Change / Cambios

Expect changes in terms of money, times, or relationships
Bringing a sense of wonder and fulfillment
What you may have consciously put on hold
Seems to fall off the shelf and into your hands

A set of old fashioned cannisters sit atop kitchen shelves. In grabbing for one, another topples over. The scattered sugar reveals a heart shaped gold bracelet that has emerged out of the fallen open cannister.

Graciella shows us the vision of the infinite possibilities of change in our lives. There are the changes we are aware of and on which we choose to focus. And yet, we are also recipients of a vast array of changes that we do not consciously prepare for but that are revealed in what seems to be an accidental manner. These are surprises that are ours, nevertheless. We may have no choice but to go with the newness whether desired or not.

At times, we become aware of an opportunity and allow its possibilities to pass us by. We blame a family member for standing in our way. We complain that we are unable to pay for a class that we've been wanting to take that suddenly appears in our Internet feed. We decide that maybe later we'll allow a desired change to take place. Not now. Why? Because we feel we aren't ready or are fearful of starting something new. Opportunities for change exist in every turn of life, however, we are the ones who determine whether they will take place or not. We may give our stagnant ideas more weight than is beneficial for us. All too frequently, we continue to do the same non-affirming things due to the familiarity and comfort level they afford.

Or we may become aware that when our inner landscape changes, we become bereft. This interior terrain may be more challenging for us to navigate than the outer. A fresh perspective comes with inner path work, and we develop, lighting our shadowed selves. We benefit by reminding ourselves of what we wanted to do before the shadows in our lives overtook us. We should ask ourselves whether we had time to even know what our dreams were.

You are encouraged to be thankful for the newness in your life. Glorious are the days that a change falls off the shelf onto your countertop, filling you with hope, faith, and compassion. These are the ingredients that make for a new you.

Reflection: When a new and wondrous change has been revealed for me, am I ready to accept it?

Affirmation: *I accept the unexpected fortunes that pour forth for me from Source.*

Contemplation / Contemplación

Contemplation is an action
Stay still in the moment
Meditate on the ever-changing patterns
All will become clear in its time

Graciella stands in a bazaar, at a table laden with fabrics of various colors and textures. Her eyes are closed, and she appears to be in a reflective state. The image evokes the tantalizing scents of perfumes and oils and of mouthwatering delicacies that are being cooked over an open fire.

We contemplate the vast array of possibilities set before us and we feel a sense of peace. Contemplation, an action, is the gift of pause. There are times that we are so impassioned by our thoughts and by our desires that we look toward a rush of manifestation of our ideas. By taking a quiet stance, by sitting in meditation, by waiting for more to be revealed, we allow ourselves to arrive at a more expansive view of the potential of our creations.

Be mindful of today's lightning-fast communications. Many of us bemoan the weeks that Mercury is in retrograde, instead of being grateful for the slowness, the opportunity for refinement of ideas, and the process of working toward clear communications. We may be irritated by the obstacles and blockages to the progress we expect. We are encouraged to utilize this time to our advantage and may find that we will be happier for it as we move closer to our goals.

There is so much going on in our world. We may be confused as to which path to take. There is no such thing as one path. All paths lead to others. There is always the possibility of turning back, changing paths yet again, including walking barefoot on the grass if that action seems right to you.

Our spiritual aspects, when strong in foundation, will ensure that we are moving in a way that is beneficial to us and our Universe. Life is mystical. In your meditation, ask to be opened to the mystery that is yours alone in Higher Power's divine nature. Contemplation affords us the ability to respond in a manner that is keeping with our highest selves. Intention and meditation are joined. The time that is afforded to contemplation transports us to other realms of reasoning with our senses. Contemplatives are purposeful in their actions and quietly manifest fulfilled spiritual lives and bring a sense of peace into the world. There is no wrong or right answer when we contemplate. We merely consider and radiate that peace of mind, soul, and spirit of self around us. We become whole.

Reflection: What things, people, and situations in my life are in the highest light and frequency? Do my wants resonate with those my Higher Power would like for me? Am I open to that conversation with my Higher Power?

Affirmation: *I am at peace as I reflect in the stillness. I am open to the fulfillment of my true self.*

Cosmos / Cosmos

The Universe is vast in relation to your being
Stand under the sparkling night sky with arms wide open
Awaken to the matching beauty within you
Sense how perfectly you fit within the constellation of the stars

Graciella stands out on a fertile green pasture in the dark of night. She gazes up to the skies appreciating the constellations and the clouds.

We each hold a special place in the Universe. Our bones are made of stardust, we are the constellations of the earth, we are the hope of the greatest things in the now and those yet to come. We have received our tradition and inner knowing from our ancestral lineages, and we pass these properties on to our children and our creations.

When we are doubtful of who we are and what we represent we should remember that there is no accident as to being in this place at this time. Just as Orion has its place in the sky, we each have our place in the Universe. While it is essential to have relationships and support systems in others, Graciella advises us not to await the words or actions of another to help us determine our rights to be here. We each have the right to be.

Look up at the skies and then look down at your feet. Observe where they are planted on the ground. Determine where you stand. It is essential for you to acknowledge your space in this Universe. Hold yourself in a wide embrace and give yourself the love that you so surely deserve. What is above, so is below. What is within is without. Never feel yourself separate, less than, or outside of the meaning and purpose of the Universe. You are here. A child of the Universe. Hold that knowledge closely to yourself.

Reflection: What messages have I received or given to myself that make me feel as though I stand apart from the love of the Universe? In what ways can I allow myself the love that I so deserve and have been withholding from myself?

Affirmation: I own my right to be here. I am blessed. I am here for a reason. I am grateful.

Dance / Baile

¡Ole! Head thrown back, arms reach up
Twisting, teasing, a snake ensnaring
Brazen like the rest who choose to dance
Your shoes tap out the sound of life's destiny

    Graciella's dancing feet, innocent and child-like in Mary Jane shoes, are dynamic in movement. The color of her full skirt is earthy green laying over petticoats of lavender and light blue hues.

    Graciella urges us to create the patterns of our own life's dance and to move our feet with all abandon. By reflecting on the steps that we've already taken, we gain insight into what prior actions have resonated with creative and joyful lives that each of us are privileged to experience. Reflect on what patterns of dance have precipitated laughter, a healthy glow, or an everlasting love. Alternately, there are dance steps that may have precipitated a fall, a sprained ankle, or a fractured relationship.

    Many of us have been taught to *sit this one out*. We stand on the sidelines as others boogie, catapult, and cha-cha their way through life. Some have slipped and fallen and have gotten up again, laughingly. They chalk up their lack of balance on spilled water, a bit of heady intoxication, or another's elbow that might have jammed into them as they sashayed onto the dance floor. You are invited to dance the dance too and to enjoy yourself. Maybe you will dance an old school version of the electric slide with your friends, the macarena at a wedding, or better yet, the chicken dance. You can be a chicken and still go forward in courage to dance your dance.

Remember though, that there is no shame in sitting out a dance if you are weary. There are those who will extend their hands to you and invite you to dance their dance. Do so, only if the dance is something that you wish to take part in. There is no need to feel pressure to do something that does not resonate with you. There are times that a person doesn't feel like dancing but eventually does take part in the festivities. The effect is one of exuberance, increased energy, and vitality. The dance may be an allegory of liberation, of truth, and of clarity.

Your dance on this earth holds promise for you and the seven generations yet to come. What does your tap, ballet, or tango bring to the world? We are more than one thing. Allow yourself to join those who dance with love in their hearts, compassion toward others, and glory in life. Graciella reminds us that life is a dance. We are encouraged to choose what type of dance fits us and in what situations. There is no need to be the proverbial wallflower. Why sit this one out? This is your life, and it is up to you to decide how you will dance.

Reflection: Am I willing to dance through the patterns of my life? Is it my time to sit on the side wings and pick up the rhythms after I've rested? I will listen to my inner voice and trust in my decision to go forward.

Affirmation: *I show up in my best form, with glee in my heart, and joy in my step.*

Darkness / Oscuridad

When darkness surrounds you
Meditate
Gradually and assuredly
Your third eye will be lit from within

    A hand gropes in the darkness. It appears to be seeking grounding as it touches the earth in its explorations.

    We emerge from the dark recesses of our Mother's womb transported into light. There are the noises, scents, sounds, and tastes we come upon. We cry and we are snuggled and swathed in love. The place of light soon becomes a place of warmth, comfort, and security. The dark becomes a place of fear, unrecognizable to us, although we were nurtured and loved in the place of shadow and intuition.

    It is often a quest for us to regain trust in the darkness. We desire the strong hand of another to guide us through the dark. But there are times that we must navigate strange places alone. With faith in our Higher Power we are encouraged to sit quietly in the dark, aware that although it may seem that we are alone we are not. In this place of shadow, we ignite the flame of a candle to produce the glimmer of light that restores our orientation.

There are times that when we are in the dark things appear so foreign that our fear overtakes us, and our surroundings appear even bleaker. Remembering who we are, in the face of a dismal period in our existence, is part of our growth and our process during our lifetimes. By acknowledging our shadow, we are then able to fully appreciate the light of our lives. Be at peace in both the dark and the light and experience the beauty of harmony and balance.

Reflection: Do my attempts at staying in the light deny me the richness of growth? Is my fear keeping me in the dark and therefore not allowing me the splendor of the light?

Affirmation: *I honor the light and the dark, knowing I require both to fulfill my existence this lifetime.*

Death / Muerte

Death as the ultimate sacrifice
Transports the soul to unexplored regions
Passing through realms in search of the new
Ensuring rebirth, restoration, and a new consciousness

    A masculine energy stands in the shadows. His countenance is somber, and he holds a weapon close to his chest.

    Death comes in many forms and as humans we often respond in fear to the idea that death is near. The image of the male seems menacing at first glance. Danger seems apparent in how he holds his weapon. We are certain that this individual is to be feared. It may be that he is the one who stands in trepidation about what is to come.

    When we are in fear of change, of transformation, of walking in eternal life, just as the image depicts, we too may stand with our backs against the wall. We may very well be on the defensive because of the uncertainty of what will transpire when we've gone through the experience of death to the old and birth to the new. Rebirth comes when we are willing to step out of the shoes we have worn for a lifetime. We may have been advised by others that we must hold on tightly to what we already know. We may be discouraged in allowing ourselves to embrace newness, not for ourselves but for those who may experience discomfort in witnessing our evolution.

Death is usually most feared in the physical, but what exactly does that mean to us? We have theories as to what we may find when we cross over into another dimension but what is needed most is faith that we will be cared for by our Higher Powers or higher good no matter what the transformational process brings to us. Spiritual, mental, and emotional transformations may be difficult to accept. Open your hearts. Open your minds. Accept the metamorphosis that belongs to you.

Reflection: Does my fear keep me from moving into other realms that my Higher Power desires for me? How can I relax my grasp and embrace all possibilities?

Affirmation: I accept myself unconditionally and am open to the transformation that my Higher Power has in store for me.

Earth / Tierra

Rejoice in the abundant gifts of the Earth
Just as She gives plentifully so must She be nourished
Feed the Earth as you would yourself
Never forget to give thanks for all that She provides

Graciella pours water and places apples and coins on the ground as offerings to the Earth.

When offering libations to the Earth we thank our home for all that it has provided for us. Just as we replenish ourselves with food and drink, the Earth requires care to continue its life and purpose. This great sphere on which we reside must be cleansed, maintained, and renewed. We are organisms, our relationship is symbiotic, and we depend on each other for harmony and balance.

We cannot continue to receive from the Earth, Gaia, the Great Mother Goddess, without returning thanks, an offering, or a gift. The Earth, as we all know, is in dire trouble. The air and the seas call for our help. There have been prophecies that foretold that these days would come. They are here now. The future still holds a very high possibility of devastation. By observing our history, we are aware of how the Earth has come to this ruination. Many of us, as humans, rip valuable resources from deep within our planet, who is our body, and our soul. We spew pollution into the air and throw toxic substances into our clear and pure waters. Fires have ravaged the vast acreage of our forest lands. We have not respected our Mother, the Earth. She will never thrive unless we treat the planet as She deserves. The Earth cannot continue as we are experiencing it today.

We are passionately urged to reflect on the ways that we may have been negligent to our beautiful Mother Earth. She encourages us to act in amending our ways. This is our home. Let us enjoy the beauty that is Her by planting, growing, cleaning, clearing, nurturing, and finally, fully loving our home.

Reflection: How have I abandoned my Earth Mother? Have I abandoned myself in similar ways?

Affirmation: *I value the Earth, my home, and act toward her healing. For I am Her and She is me.*

The East / El Este

The new day brings illumination
Vast and wondrous
Open your heart and mind
Accept the knowing

A rowboat is set in a pond surrounded by cattails and trees still seemingly barren. The glow of the rising sun is observed in the background.

The east brings us awakenings. It inspires us to move ahead in thanks that we have lived to see another day on our planet, Earth. We are encouraged to look to the light of the East for answers, visions, and remedies for our ailments. Many traditions point to the East for direction, purpose, and prayer. We are assured that wisdom, and knowledge will be attained when we fully give ourselves to trusting in the clarity that the East provides.

Pursuing truths sometimes reveals our fears or confirmation that our discomforts are founded. How one proceeds with the information received is a choice. Will I respond in remorse or violence or profound sadness? Will I regret my request for clarity? How can I manage acute awareness while remaining in kindness and in solidarity with my higher self. How can I walk in the way of the wise?

Be aware of information that will soon be revealed. We may not be astounded by what we hear, yet instead be comforted that all is not illusion. We may be relieved to know that what we may have suspected is confirmed. There are many days and nights that we are in a limbo-like existence. We may have an intuition or a thought that what we perceive is a reality and we must bide our time until that information is announced in a forthright manner. As intuitives and perceptives we are encouraged to believe in our hunches, but still as humans we would like to have confirmation of these knowings. Be on the lookout for a revelation. It may come in casual conversation, the mail, or via a media outlet. Better yet, turn to the East in your early morning meditation. Open to what you experience with your senses. Be assured that the information that is for you will come.

Reflection: I have faced the East and prayed for the revelations that are meant for me. How will I respond to my awakened state as I make my way out into the world?

Affirmation: *I am open to the knowledge that is afforded to me today.*

Fear / Temor

Anxiety claims space in your being
Dread is merely a projection
Willingly surrender with breath
Consciously release with love

Graciella leaves the manor behind. She is carrying what appears to be a heavy disk. Her face shows anxiety and dread.

Fear is a human trait that is shared by all. It is manifested by some as anger, a sense of paralysis, fatigue, and by others as mere apprehension. These various forms of fear are not aligned with an individual's true sense of being or potential. Fear comes in all shapes and sizes. It is like water and squeezes into all openings. It is like air, and we easily catch it from someone in our environment. It is like fire and consumes us until we collapse into ashes. It is like parched earth that doesn't easily yield. Fear is one of humanity's driving forces. We need not be enslaved by it.

We miss opportunities that we have been afforded that are within our reach when we respond in fear. We become irritable or dangerous toward others because we are fearful and intolerant of our differing beliefs.

We turn away from our fellow humans because we are uneasy and frightened by what we don't understand.

When fear is recognized, we can move with courage, like a stealth ninja, reclaiming our peace, our rights, our love. Changing fear to love is an action that is life changing. By doing this we can see truths, sit in discomfort, and seek to move beyond what we already think we know. By objectively sitting with our fear and misaligned actions, we can observe their effects on our higher calling as human beings.

Reflection: How do my fear-based decisions keep me from responding to myself and to others with love? How does that influence the life I wish for myself?

Affirmation: *I allow my love to overtake my fear.*

Fertility / Fertilidad

Life is rich with promise
Expectant with the great possibilities
The Creator has tailored especially for you
Keep steady as your potentials are realized

A purple pouch lies on the ground against rocks and grasses. A few gold coins and a necklace have fallen from the pouch.

When most individuals contemplate fertility, the concepts of pregnancy and birth are not far behind. There are many types of pregnancies and birthings. Congratulations to all of you who may be moving toward the birth of a child and to those who are progressing in their gestation toward the birthing of a creative project.

Know that you are fertile and have personal and sacred gifts to bring onto this Earth. They may not be what you anticipated. We are often surprised about the turns our creative lives take. Know that you are celebrated for birthing your gifts as promised this lifetime.

For each of us, there are periods of gestation. We are given, in some cases, exact parameters of time.

Those of us who have held a living developing being in our wombs have been advised that the nine-month gestation period is essential for the birth of a healthy baby. Gestation and the need for patience may not be so apparent in our other creative works. There are always an infinite number of details that must be attended to before a creation is birthed into the world. Are you listening to the needs of your project or only to your will? Do you feel rushed in creating a plot for your novel or in writing your memoir? Does the house you have been saving for still seem out of reach?

We may feel the urge to birth a product before its due date. It may seem that others are busily manifesting while our projects remain stagnant. We are not aware of the processes of others. It would do us some good to concentrate on our creations and not those of others. Allow your relationship with your creation to slowly develop and be birthed in its due time. Know that the time for a fertile and rich creation is individualized.

Reflection: Communicate with your creation and listen to its response. You may be surprised at the abundance that your creation hopes to bring you.

Affirmation: My creative center is blessed, and I manifest beauty in this world.

Fidelity / Fidelidad

Loyal to the situation to a fault
Is it commitment or conformity?
Are you faithful to yourself or to others' expectations?
Be brave!

    Graciella stands before a cross in the road. She is cloaked in deep purple and extends a white lily in front of her. The moon casts its light in the sky.

    We are faced with a decision of which road is most true to our authentic self. When faced with the choice of being true to one's ideals many of us will toss our heads and declare, *I know which path is mine and I will never stray from that path.* That is the value that we like to believe is ours. To have such strength of character is one wished for but might not truly exist despite our dreams and desires. We grow and we change. What may be our path today changes when we come to the inevitable fork in the road. The question of whether we continue as we have or whether it is time to take a turn sits before us. We pause as we reflect on our choices, knowing that only when we take the next step will more information be revealed.

Sometimes it's hard to see what keeps us stuck. We hold on despite our misgivings that the path we have chosen may no longer be worthy of who we are today. Many of us are reared to be loyal to a fault. We hold onto our traditions, mores, and cultures, but in our hearts our convictions shift, and we are stirred to do things differently. Deep resounding change may be unfamiliar to us. Others change around us, but we are resistant to give up what no longer serves us, or to what or who no longer offers us the compassionate way of life.

Be true to thyself. Fidelity is about love, it is about veracity, it is about keeping one's head with dignity and honor. Fidelity is also about compromise, no matter what we choose or believe to be the right path. Others have made their choices by enacting the concept of fidelity on their own terms and we are reminded to accept others' choices with grace.

Reflection: Am I in fear of the actions I'd like to take? Will I hurt myself? Will I harm someone else? Am I acting with compassion and love?

Affirmation: *As I stand at the crossing on the middle road, I remain true to my authentic self as I know it today. I rely on the hands of love and compassion as I decide which road to take.*

Fire / Fuego

Offer fire the respect it has earned since creation
Listen to its hiss and feel the scorch of its kiss
Gaze deeply into the embers to discern
Spirit and the sacredness of life

The flames of the fire show images that can be easily discerned by the naked eye. We see dancing figures, a heart, and a footprint amongst others.

We equate fire with passion and intuition. With fire's intensity we can create, love, feel, act, and progress. Fire is also known to be destructive and can devour everything in its path. Know that balance is necessary when working with the element of fire. We are encouraged to engage in practicing balance when impassioned or obsessed with a particular quest. Fire could produce a high level of energy that tells us we don't need harmony and balance and that we should allow our sparks to ignite, and our flames spread.

Fire is an element of transformation or transmutation that changes eternally. It can be quite intimidating when close to it. We are astonished by the almost unbearable beauty of fire in its liquid form of lava. Fire can be used as a boundary to keep ourselves separate from people and environments. Fire can be contained with close monitoring, but it can also begin to destroy what is in reach in a split second. Fire steps in to rid forests of shrubbery and trees that need to be removed for new growth. Unless one is affected by fire there is truly no understanding of its power.

    Become acquainted with fire by lighting a candle or building a flame in a fireplace or a fire pit. Sit before it and scry the flames or the embers of this sacred fire. See and feel the images that are shown to you and observe how they are relevant in your life. Listen to its hiss and its hum. Communicate with fire and build your personal relationship with it. Mostly, show fire the utmost respect it deserves as sacred life.

Reflection: Do I allow my soul to stoke the flames of fire? Am I in fear of its transformational aspects, as well as my intuitions? Am I in right relationship with fire or do I dampen its existence in my life?

Affirmation: *The flame I sit before opens my eyes to the metamorphosis of life. I honor the flame of my spirit.*

Fool / Tonto

Believing what easily comes is yours for the keeping
Reflect on the actions you are about to make
They may bring discomfort and distress
And your life could become a cautionary tale

A masculine energetic being has literally been caught in oncoming headlights as he reaches for treasure hidden in a pond. A rabbit sits alert to the situation.

We muse over the idea of whether the treasure was stolen or belongs to the person reaching for it. The belief that hidden actions are unseen is a false one. There is always someone watching. Eyes come in many forms and may not be visible to one's own eyes. Observers may be outside forces or one's own inner forces. In this image, the male, or individual of yang characteristics, does not seem to have been adequately prepared for the unfolding of events that are about to occur.

If fool energy abounds there are several questions to ponder. The first is whether the energy is coming from the surroundings or being emitted by the questioner. What were the circumstances leading to the pulling of this card? The answer may be as simple as someone entangling themselves in a situation in which they have no business.

Everyone has been foolish at one time or another. There is no need for our egos to become dismantled if something is done clumsily, in error, or if others witness an action that might have been done differently. Egoists may strike out in mortal fear of being found foolish. There is a difference in feelings resulting from being caught versus feelings resulting from taking that action.

At still a deeper level, a fool is most likely unaware of their lack of knowledge. There is a simplicity in unknowing and becoming an open vessel for love and understanding. We walk on this planet sometimes in uncertainty and at other times self-assured of our knowledge about what was, what is, and what is to come. When pulling this card, putting yourself on pause may be useful. You are encouraged to sit in ignorance and to reflect on illuminating light that may fill you with knowledge and wisdom.

Allow yourself time to respond in a responsible manner and not to react to difficult situations inflamed by fear.

Reflection: I will take a moment to contemplate the actions I have taken that add to our thick cosmic soup and remember that humility may be defined as being teachable.

Affirmation: *I forgive myself and release my regrets. I am my best friend and treat myself in that manner.*

Fortune Teller / Adivinadora

*Seek outside counsel
Scry water, throw runes, dream with your crystal sphere
Know your fortune, know your future*

Graciella is seated at a table set with a card spread. We are unaware of whether Graciella is giving or receiving the reading. The picture on the far wall shows a bright outdoor scene that contrasts with the indoor dimness. There is a large sleeping black dog, symbolic of loyalty, lying on the floor. An armoire is filled with potions and notions.

The Fortune Teller comes in many faces. We query the woman who sits in her window beckoning us to come into her storefront. We are confronted with displays of crystals, geodes, and spheres. There may be pyramid replicas. These remind us of something within us that may have long been neglected or once tended to that has been forgotten in the daily stream of life.

The invitation to access a reading with a divinator is an invitation to walk within ourselves and the rooms that we hold within our being. A fortune teller may come in the form of a clairvoyant, clairaudient, a scryer, a tarot reader, or someone who throws runes or bones. There are many forms of divination. By accessing the assistance of a divinator, we are saying yes to accessing that which is in ourselves. When we open to receiving clarity to our obscure thoughts or outright confusion, we are provided with remedies that will help us resolve the issues we've brought forth.

When determining whether a particular reader is one that can be trusted with your intimate information, check within. What do your senses tell you? Are your guides encouraging you or are you feeling doubtful? Listen to your intuition. If you experience a feeling of reluctance in your gut, you may want to seek out another reader. Does the reader resonate with you? Continue with the process with trust and proceed accordingly. As in all situations, if you are uncomfortable you may leave with grace.

This card may also be a message for you to become familiar with the various divination tools of your heritage. If you are attracted to using runes in your practice although they are not associated with your lineage, go ahead anyway. You may be working with a guide who has something new to teach you. The runes may have been your divination tool in one of your past lives.

The tool we are always encouraged to hone is the one of intuition. There is no reaching out for decks, bones, shells, or other devices that we use as oracles in our quests for answers. We always have access to intuition. By consistently meditating, we sharpen the tool of divination that we hold within. We do ourselves and our lives a disservice by not meditating. Just as bathing or feeding ourselves daily, meditation brings us a shiny, fulfilled, and awakened sense of self. If you are not meditating, ask yourself why you choose not to make time to care for your spiritual self. Meditation comes in many forms. Your manner of meditating may be taking a walk, a jog, or closing your door for a five-minute interval of quiet. How we choose to meditate belongs to us. Some of us can sit quietly for an hour and others do well with a few minutes at a time. Here as well, to thine own self be true.

Reflection: I am blind to answers that I seek. Where can I access guidance for my higher good and for those that I serve?

Affirmation: I am here for my higher good, and to fulfill the path I was born to walk. I ask for guidance.

Friendship / Amistad

Reveling in similarities
Celebrating differences
Never to be forgotten and often to be forgiven
Friendship is the cornerstone of love and life

A gold bracelet laden with charms lays against a background of purple, reminiscent of velvet, that is strewn with a sprinkling of lavender stars.

There are many levels of friendship, and each is divinely touched. Friendship is about love, loyalty, and patience, as well as creating boundaries if required. Our charge in maintaining solid bonds with others means being available for them while also allowing ourselves the right to limit our time and energy to keep ourselves healthy. Honesty and transparency with others are key to maintaining friendships. Compassion is the overarching theme to be mindful of in our bonds with our friends but also with ourselves. If we embody these concepts, we may find that we have more to share with individuals we call friends.

When we assess the quality of our relationships we must be brutally or gently honest with ourselves regarding our expectations. Do we have high standards for others and then pull back when it is our turn to be the friend who is needed? Our default mode may be one of leaning into our relationships for support. Or we may isolate ourselves from those who would like to be the pillars we stand against during difficult times. Have we allowed our misguided or dysfunctional beliefs about friendship, limit setting, loyalty, or betrayal seep into our expectations of our friends and relations? Do we fine that we flee from certain relationships because we find ourselves drained by the interactions. Take time to think about whether you have been the friend that can be counted on. Have you allowed another to be the friend that you desire? Ask yourself, are you being a friend to yourself. The goal is to have healthy attachments.

Everyone has their own path, experience, and personal knowledge. While developing a healthy stance for yourself, allow your fellow ties to determine what is healthy for them. By accepting liberation and self-determination, you may find yourself going toward a progressive friendship on a path you both choose.

Reflection: Have I tilled the soil of my relationships so that love and compassion circulate underneath its foundation, creating a balance and harmony desired and sustainable for both of us?

Affirmation: I honor you and myself as I tend to our rich and beautiful friendship.

Gatherer / Recolectora

*Gather for wholeness, sustenance, and need
Leave behind doubt of future provision
Have faith that you will always be provided for in this lifetime
Know with a joyful heart that your prayers have been answered*

A woven basket is filled with bright pink flowers. The basket is set in a garden of lush greenery. There is a bull's horn on the ground.

Throughout our lives we gather perceptions, thoughts, emotions, and materials. It is prudent to take periodic stock of things accumulated. The beginning of a year, in whatever your tradition or lineage, is commonly a time for evaluation. It is essential to assess the items fully before determining whether they are still needed or no longer fruitful. Many of us gather baskets filled with worry. Expectations and urgencies are the usual precursors to worry. Letting things evolve naturally allows us to empty our baskets.

Honesty is important to our appraisals. Did we amass not what we needed but what we wanted? What was delighted in and what did you wish you had never received? Is there a feeling of deprivation, or do you lack gratitude for what you have? Graciella reminds us that whatever is meant for us will come to us if we have faith and persist in our work toward that which we desire. As the bull's horn depicts, allow the Earth's elements, your persistence, your actions, and collection of life's experiences bolster your fortitude.

Graciella urges us not to be overly concerned that we will have to do without. Have faith that prayers are answered and there is no need to ruminate on the needs that you determined are yours. Ask for and work toward what you believe is yours. Remember that your Higher Power may have different ideas of what you should have or a timetable that is not what you have in mind. Be assured that you will obtain and attain what is truly yours.

Baskets have many openings. As you gather, introspect on what you may be wasting, what may be seeping through the cracks, and what will fill your basket that ensures you not only survival, but provides abundance and prosperity in your life.

Reflection: What does my basket hold? What have I placed into it? Do the items I've accumulated reflect myself and my desires for this lifetime?

Affirmation: *I persist, and I persevere as I work toward filling my basket with what I desire. I turn my basket of worries upside down and watch them fly off like butterflies. I transform.*

The Gypsy / La Gitana

Tambourine jingling; guitar strumming
Hair blowing in the breeze
A legend of desire
Aware of your identity; keep the mystery

Graciella is in celebration fully enjoying herself in music, dance, and company. Her beloved parrot is at her side. The masculine aspect shares the artistry of music. He only has eyes for the gypsy, Graciella.

The gypsy has earned her freedom and is taking full pleasure in celebration. When the feminine and masculine aspects of our beings are united, we can share ourselves deeply with abandon. Graciella encourages us to allow ourselves to be. We are not disposed to the thoughts and feelings of others. While we may listen or even tolerate other points of view, they may not take root nor destroy the peace and joy we hold within.

No one, except for our familiar, the parrot in this case, knows the heartache, grief, and pain that has been endured unless we've chosen to share our stories. We may decide to keep the mystery of our lives close to our hearts and not share it with the world.

The outside world has no judgment on our lives. We have no judgments on theirs.

There may be others who are interested or curious as to the joy that emanates from within us. We inspire them in our clever and bodacious ways. Our beauty is inspiring and contagious, yet we are still allowed to keep our innermost worlds private. We share what we choose and that is one's perfect right to maintain peace and jubilation in our lives.

Reflection: Do I allow myself to fully be me without succumbing to the projected needs of others? How do I maintain relationships while honoring myself?

Affirmation: *I am in the fullness and strength I have gathered throughout my lifetimes.*

Health / Salud

Well-being encompasses the many levels of your being
Physical, mental, emotional, and spiritual
Attend to all aspects and achieve
a healthy and harmonious balance

Graciella sits on the bed next to a person who is unwell. She offers soup and a listening ear and brings a spiritual context to the situation. There are fresh herbs and a religious icon on the wall. The colors of the blanket are rich. The soup is sure to be a broth that was made with love.

At first glance, it appears that a woman is tending to a man who is injured or ill. That may be, but it may also be that the feminine nature of the individual is tending to their own masculine nature. The gentle, seemingly passive, side of ourselves influences the assertive and dominant ways that sometimes overtake us.

Health is necessary for a life well-lived. Health encompasses the physical, mental, emotional, and spiritual aspects of ourselves. Balancing all of these domains moves us closer to general well-being than when we focus on only one or two of these aspects in our lives. Use this time to determine the condition of these domains. Working from the inside out is a profound path for healing. Often, we look to the outside for approval, recognition, and advice. While these measures are helpful, we are encouraged to intuit and to pay heed to the inner knowing. As we ask ourselves what aspects need healing, we are urged to truly listen.

This card may also ask us to consider growing our spiritual selves. We may have been turned off by what were the religions or our parents' or guardians' concepts of health and spirituality, or a lack thereof, when we were children. Our spiritual lives and health practices do not belong to our parents. They are ours and ours alone. What is the foundation made of that prompts you to say that you walk on a spiritually healthy path?

Reflection: I reflect on what may service my health needs. How can I be open to growth and change within a healthy framework for my life or maybe that of a dear loved one?

Affirmation: I am blessed with health and healing. I am open to the healing energies that the Universe abundantly provides for me. In prayer and compassionate love, I pray for your healing as well as mine.

Impasse / Punto Muerto
Decisions that seem to be between life and death are not
You have options; therefore, choices to make
Set objectives and goals, make plans
Steer away from getting stuck at the fork in the road

A figure stands directly opposite a herd of bulls. We note that the figure is wearing a suit and hat that is an unlikely outfit on the grassy terrain. Beyond the herd, we see that the sun is posed to illuminate the cloudy sky. The image is also suggestive of the crescent moon. The grounds flourish while the trees are barren.

We are uncertain if the man is guiding the herd which seems doubtful in his suit and hat or if he encounters these as living obstacles as he walks toward a destination or goal. This masculine aspect has options. Faced against this grazing herd, he can turn around and forge another path. If it is his herd and he is experienced, he will well know how to have the animals follow him. If he needs to go another way to meet his goal, he can feel confident about his travel as the signs around him tell him it is a go.

There are reasons for the obstructions on our paths. Sometimes we encounter them to practice our tools of patience and perseverance. Take a moment to pause and reflect on the circumstance surrounding your experienced impasse. There may be excellent justification for it although the block was unforeseen. When we feel that we have come to an impasse at any point in a situation we take a step aside, not back, to observe and assess. We reflect on our surroundings. We are advised not to get stuck with what stands before us. There is always a way to meet our challenges and to continue toward the manifestation of our intentions.

What may be keeping you at a standstill today might very well be rooted in the past. How many of us are eager to dig deep and find the causes that may still be very present in our lives today? Although our pasts may keep us at a point of impasse, we can decide whether we will choose to use the keys of our knowledge to unlock the doors we have thus far been unable to open. Whether we need the help of others or decide to take these actions on our own, opening the doors is something worth considering.

Reflection: Today is an opportunity for me to meditate on the light of the sun that breaks through my clouds. I envision that the impasse before me will yield in its own time.

Affirmation: *I am in faith that when it is my time, along with my works, obstructions that stand before me will be removed.*

Intimacy / Intimidad
Acknowledge your feelings
Communicate your desires and boundaries
With loyalty to the self
The capacities in this partnering surpass any expectation

The yin and yang figures lay nude next to each other in the dark. Their eyes are closed, and they are both slightly smiling.

The word intimacy has the same root as intimidate. To be intimate may indeed be intimidating for many of us. What is appropriate or comfortable for one person may not be for another. We are encouraged to be patient as we learn the ways of openness and creating a healthy bond with those we choose to have in our lives, as well as with ourselves.

There are many ways for us to develop our abilities to be close to others. The process of intimacy is one that we work on throughout our many lifetimes. These cycles of life can be viewed in our current human states or through a perspective that each time our spirits choose a human framework in which to work we continuously evolve. While acknowledging the power of intergenerational influence on our abilities to develop relationships, we focus on the primary ones beginning with our care providers during infancy, whether biological or otherwise. As we mature and deepen our sense of self, we eventually question the actions of those principal life defining relationships and their consequences. With guidance and love, we can establish our separate identities and seek to fulfill our promises from a chosen perspective.

The intimacy we create with ourselves is fundamental. Many of us attempt to grow healthy bonds with others when we don't even truly know ourselves. The development of an intimate relationship with ourselves is essential if we are to contemplate growing a healthy relationship with another. Upon waking each morning, embrace yourself in love. Know that you can always depend upon the love from you to you.

Love the child, the adolescent, and the young adult within you. Once you have acknowledged and honored those parts of yourself, you may be open to the deep enrichment of a relationship with another. The process may be slow. The healing is profound.

Reflection: What are the expectations I have of another that only I can fulfill for myself? In what ways can I attend to the inner me that will allow me to open my heart even more than it is today?

Affirmation: *My relationship with myself is one of trust, clarity, and security. In loving myself I can love another.*

Kindness / Caridad

There is sweetness in the giving
No expectation of reward
The gain is in the service
A steppingstone for liberation of the self

Hands hold a flower in front of the ebb and flow of the tide. The ocean froth on the sand shows the elusive quality of the act of kindness.

Balance of the self is experienced when we intuitively know when to give and when we are in need of receiving acts of compassion. Just as the ocean waters ebb and flow so there is rhythm to these actions in our lives. Although we extend acts of kindness without a price or expectation of acknowledgment, we are aware that the Universe notices our acts of love. We are reminded to engage in acts of kindness when it may not be the first thought that has come to us.

There may be times that we seethe with resentments. We ruminate on all the ways that we can plot revenge on someone who we believe deserves retribution. It may be that those who are harmed in times of unvoiced anger may indeed only be ourselves. We are encouraged to process our feelings and to move forward so that we aren't left with bitterness that may permeate all aspects of our lives. Holding on to the sting of resentment does not serve our higher purpose. We should not deny our feelings or avoid them or soar past them, and we are cautioned against getting mired in them.

Forgiveness is an instrument of faith that many forget or hesitate to give others. Forgiving others allows us to forgive ourselves. By diving deeply into the oceans of forgiveness, compassion, and love we are offered the gifts of releasing angers, old and new, that no longer serve us.

The power of kindness extends beyond the reach of anything that we can understand as humans. There are goddesses in many religions that embody motherhood, caring, and a sense of nurturance and well-being to their devotees. Compassion raises the violet light of transmutation of energies toward health and healing for ourselves and the collective. The environment is us and we are the environment. The Universes harmonize with love that is extended to all beings in every form whenever anyone engages in an act of kindness.

Reflection: Kindness is freely available and within reach. Do I allow myself to receive such goodness? What would my life be like if I were to also extend it to others without condition?

Affirmation: *I am kind and gentle with myself, allowing me to be freely compassionate to another. I wholeheartedly enter the cycle of kindness.*

Lament / Llanto

Weep
Release the wretched sorrow you hold within
The distress will fade when acknowledged
And its power will dissolve

Graciella sits close to the ground with her head hung low. There is an owl on a branch of a bare tree. The full moon and the pyramids are in the background. A colorful snake and brightly colored flowers are on the ground close to Graciella's body.

Shedding tears is one of the greatest tools for the release of our deepest sorrows. The owl of wisdom and the snake of transmutation are witnesses to the profound sadness exuded by the feminine principle. The barrenness of the tree is contrasted by the full warmth and nurturance of the moon. The flowers show the beauty that is nearby for Graciella to see, if only she would lift her head. By allowing ourselves to feel our most profound sadnesses and releasing them, we give space for newness in our lives. There are many individuals who are in deep pain and grief, who are filled with sorry and regret. Loss of work, homes, and necessities have us wondering what will come next that we may be unable to control. We may be experiencing the pain of the loss of someone we've had deep love for, and we may be in the midst of bewilderment as we consider the loss of life as we once experienced it.

Graciella encourages us to allow ourselves to feel and to be. Speaking with a trusted individual about our innermost troubles may help as well as praying aloud to one's Higher Power. Once we shed our tears, we may be open to the beauty of the messages that we hear. Messages come in many forms. We are urged to look up and out of the darkness that permeates our souls.

There may be fear that if we allow tears to run down our cheeks they will never stop. Just like everything in the seasons of our lives, there are ends and beginnings to the cycles of life, of happiness, sadness, and all things experienced. Once we lift our heads from sorrow, the transformation we have experienced is revealed. Thoroughly lamenting a painful situation opens the doors to infinite possibilities. By entering deeply into our emotions and sitting with them for as long as we truly need, we can then transform.

Reflection: By acknowledging my pain and my sorrow, I will have the ability to revel in the joy and peace that have been inside me quietly awaiting their time to emerge.

Affirmation: *I honor the sadness that has gathered in my soul. I sit with it and value the healing that it brings me.*

Madam / Madama

With confidence earned over a lifetime
Your chest swells with pride
Throw your wrap over your shoulders
Beware of what you project

Graciella is toasted in celebration as she walks down the steps in a state of pride. Behind her, at the top of the stairs, are figures also wearing ballroom dresses.

Graciella's bearing shows experience and wisdom that have been gathered from lifetimes. We need not fear the power that exudes from our beings. We are meant to be aware of the inner collections of our understandings. We acknowledge them, feel them deeply, and share them with others. We celebrate ourselves by not keeping our earned wisdom from others, instead we offer it to those who have chosen to walk with us on our paths for times yet undetermined.

There are different ways that we impart our experience to others. We decide ways which are comfortable for us, whether it be by our carriage, our words, our arts, or our industries. What is most important is that we share optimism and that we take care not to belittle others who are not like-minded.

We have all needed mentors, and we remember those who have been teachers for us and how they made us feel as they imparted their knowledge. Did we feel hurt by the aggressions in how we were advised? Did we feel love and compassion from our mentors? Did we think of our wisdom keepers as powers of example in a negative or positive way? Were they open to what we were able to teach them in reciprocal relationship? These questions will aid us in shaping how we communicate as we now give to others just as we have received.

Reflection: When I share my experience, do I remember, reflect, and act accordingly? Do I offer respect to those on my path, or do I exert my will and not that of the compassionate Universe? Am I open to a reciprocal relationship?

Affirmation: *I am a channel for the kind wisdom of the Universe.*

Moon / Luna

Celebrate the beauty and intuition of the Feminine
Lift your arms in prayer to the Great Goddess
Whether waxing, waning, or during dark of the Moon
Your incisive perception emanates
from the knowing deep within

Graciella extends her arms to the moon and converses with that which rules the tides, the energies of the feminine, and the phases of our mysteries. The sphinx is in the distance holding the secrets of ages.

Graciella reminds us that the moon is always up in the sky whether she shows her full face, is smiling at us, or is in her dark mystery that we are unable to discern with our human eyes. We can feel her energies and we attune ourselves to her. We, as a people, have become attuned to the significance of the full moon. We participate in full moon rituals, moon circles, moon prayers, and moon meditations. Graciella suggests that we become even more aware of the cycles of the moon in our daily lives.

There are several phases of the moon. We are encouraged to become more deeply acquainted with the ebbs and flows of shadow dancing with light both in the skies and in our beings. Do we intuitively know when it is most auspicious to begin or end a project? Are there days that we are being encouraged to do nothing at all? Are we aware of what days and nights that we should consider setting aside for celebration? Have we personally created a relationship with the moon?

We are encouraged to refrain from engaging in activities of planning during the exact time of the new moon. This is a time of quiet, of pause, of patience. The darkness and confusion that may ensue during true moon dark tells us it is not the time to begin new projects. Once the glimmer of the moon is observable, that is the time to engage in planning for newness in our lives. Discover the patterns of the moon's waxing and waning phases. We may save ourselves much frustration and turmoil if we balance our inner working with those of Grandmother Moon who profoundly loves us.

Reflection: Am I in balance with the energies of Grandmother Moon? Do I allow myself to be in all shades of the light and the dark? Am I open to the cycles of my feminine nature? Do I blame my unrest on those cycles, or have I looked within?

Affirmation: Grandmother Moon, I listen to your messages of love with all my heart, my soul, and my being.

North / Norte

The North speaks to you of the past
The elders impart their wisdom
Sharing history through pictures and words
Providing comfort and understanding

A fortress is hidden amongst the snow-covered mountains. Trees surround a deep lake filled with blue water. There are eight flags on the fortress waving in the wind.

The North is reminding us to be in gratitude for the bountiful gifts that have come our way through the arduous walk of those preceding us on this land. Those that prepared and nurtured the soil for us and the ones who surrendered their souls and bodies so that we may flourish. Give thanks for your ancestors and all they have given for the future generations that have come and are still yet to come. Inhale intention of your prayer of thanks. Exhale its manifestation in the Universe.

It's imperative, especially for those of us living on turtle island, to pay homage to the north, to the old ones and those gone by. The ancestors are accessible to all of us two-leggeds on this planet as we face the

North and feel its energies. We aren't destined to walk alone on this road. Although for many of us they are not visible, our ancestors have been through much of what we are going through now and would like to help us. The elders who have crossed over are in appreciation when they hear us call their names aloud. Apply a small touch of honey on your tongue and lips as you ask for their relationship and for their love.

By remembering the hurts, pains, and injuries either within this life or in a previous life we can begin to heal. We are reminded that we may feel as though we are reliving past painful moments, but we are not. They are memories that we honor for the teachings that remain with us.

Sit with your face to the North. Listen to the messages that come to you. Observe the visions that you view with your third eye and feel with your heart. Be gentle with yourself as you take in the information. It is not meant to hurt. It is meant to heal. Kadeeshday. You are made beautiful.

Reflection: How do I honor the past, the place of the old ones, those gone by? In what ways should I continue to work with what I've been taught by the elders and how shall I incorporate what I've learned into my wisdom?

Affirmation: *I listen to the messages of the North and their energies of wisdom merge with mine.*

Opportunity / Oportunidad

Fortuitously, opportunity abounds
Ready to take the chance
Ready to take the risk
What do you have to lose? Or gain?

Dice and chips lie against a green felt table. Graciella seizes the opportunity and throws the dice, taking a chance.

Graciella tells us to take heed of the old sayings, *Life is a Gamble, Strike while the Iron is Hot, and Opportunity Knocks but Once.* During our lives, we are often provided with veiled opportunities to make changes in our lives that would be beneficial for us. Because the offer is not spoken in an outright manner, we are unsure of how to proceed. The introverted or timid may be afraid to speak up. Low self-esteem and fear may inhibit others from assertively requesting what might be theirs. A request for clarity in many cases would suffice to get our messages across to the one who is extending a somewhat oblique offer.

There are other possibilities that are offered in more overt manners. An individual is encouraged to consider options that they have never contemplated.

Others have observed them to be the perfect individual for a job or candidate for a post, but they respond reticently to the proposition. It can be that an individual becomes aware of a chance for progress or accomplishment in their personal or professional life, yet they hesitate in going forward to lay claim to the prospect.

Reflect on what may be yours if only you ask for it. What is the worst possible thing that could happen by being forthright and by plainly asking for what you desire? Will you be refused or worse yet, ridiculed? Those resulting consequences are unlikely; however, you are being encouraged to be vulnerable in asking for something that may be meaningful for you. Know that you are your best representative and get to work. Ask for what you believe is rightfully yours. You may be pleased that you did. What do you have to lose?

Reflection: Although I am aware of my positive characteristics and my abilities, do I deny myself opportunities that have presented themselves to me?

Affirmation: I lay claim to the possibilities that cross my path and allow fate and my Higher Power to determine the outcome.

Patience / Paciencia

Despite your beliefs that the timing is right
What you desire is not yet ready for fruition
Be patient in this situation
The wait will strengthen your resolve

A young male patiently awaits Graciella who engages in hanging laundry to dry. While he may seem indifferent, the general tone of the card is one of light-heartedness and levity. The small white dog barks as though inviting the male to play.

As individuals we hope that situations will change. That what we desire will come forth on our timetable. Graciella urges us to review the history of events, to reflect on how we may best be of service, and to take right action as we wait. She encourages us to go with the flow of the breeze that ruffles our feathers and scatters our plans. She suggests we take our time and not make hasty decisions in situations large and small.

Those who have expectations for quick outcomes are apt to be in anguish or fretfulness at the slowness of awaited results. The desire for favorable news or an unnatural swift solution in a situation often brings with it unneeded worry.

We are a people who have become used to instant gratification. Long gone are the days of waiting for a letter or a mailman on horseback to bring awaited news! The Universe is splendid in timing, much better than we are. By being open to a Higher Power or Higher Purpose, we allow for the ripening of what we crave. We are afforded this time of waiting to engage in areas that may need completion prior to our longed for wish to manifest.

We may be in a hurry to get our tasks and chores quickly completed to sit with a good book at the end of the day. We rush through the responsibilities we don't particularly love. Are we able to truly enjoy the novel or the story? Or have we exhausted ourselves because we spent the day toiling? Instead of completely decluttering the closet now, spend a planned amount of time at it and an equal amount of time reading a book.

Waiting for the anticipated ending may mean that we aren't able to fully appreciate it when it comes. We become tired or lose interest. The excitement of anticipation sadly turns to apathy. As either the one waiting or the one engaged in seemingly endless activity, reflect on how you can best balance the situation.

Reflection: Today I sit in prayer and patience knowing that when the time is right, that which is for me will manifest. How may I best use this time fruitfully?

Affirmation: *I am worthy of waiting for what I deserve. I am of value and do not rush forward. I am certain that my time will come when it is truly my time.*

Position / Posición

Above you, below you, before you, behind you
Shift your gaze to each of these positions
Centered and grounded
Experience your world safely and assuredly

Graciella stands in front of a wheel of fortune whose colors are vivid. Her carriage is sassy. Visible on the wheel are the words love and fear.

Graciella reminds us that we are in the center of our own Universe. We each have different histories, perspectives, and perceptions. Determine where you stand in your Universe. What lies to the right and to the left of you? What lies behind you and in front of you? Don't forget to assess what lies below you and above you. Take time for reflection and you will be able to ascertain your place in the world and to take action from a stance of trust within yourself.

The word that Graciella shares with positioning is prudence. Good judgment and common-sense factor in this concept. Don't be dismayed by the root word, prude. Unfortunately, the word has been used negatively. It is a misconception that prudes don't have fun. There are many happy-go-lucky people who are content with their lives who have established a firm bedrock upon which they enjoy lives filled with joy and celebration.

Graciella encourages us not to become caught between love and fear. There are shades in between. Matters are not limited to black and white. Or hot and cold. Or midnight and noon. We spend more of our existences in the gray, in the tepid, in the in-between times. Get to know your multiple positions within the extremes. A profound knowledge of self allows us flexibility and the ability to move toward a stable foundation in our lives.

Reflection: What are the strengths that fire up my core? When I am pulled outside of myself and the depths of my convictions, how do I choose to interact in the world in a manner that is true to me? Do I give over to chance? Do I realize the depth of who I am?

Affirmation: *I live a life filled with love. Love is always the answer.*

Poverty / Pobreza

Poverty is laced with a sense of pride
When your reality is no longer fruitful
There is yet more to be released
Only then will you move forward

Graciella holds a gold bracelet in her hand. She gazes in what seems to be a distressed manner at a pawn shop window. Looking back at her, we see a man in the storefront window standing behind a guitar and what appears to be a ruby ring.

There are times that we feel as though we have nothing left and yet we must give up even more to survive. A sense of pride tells us that we should have done better, and we may be surprised at the depths to which we believe we have descended. But what is pride when we are in survival mode? Feeding ourselves, residing in secure and comfortable places, and being adequately clothed are our priorities.

Graciella is telling us that though we may find there is more to release, this is only a temporary state. Some of what we have released will indeed return when the timing is right for us. Having faith that things are as they should be is how we can temper our emotions during this time of desolation. Know that you are a child of the Universe and sing your name out in prayer. Listen as you hear your name echoed back to you with love.

Graciella asks us to reflect on what we mourn most? Is it love or objects? For whom and what purpose were these items truly meant? What do we feel we have lost? Are we in debt over a lifestyle, choices made, or a past that no longer fits our current reality? Go forward and envision what you would have in your future. Has this experience changed your perspective, or do you remain distraught over what may have been an illusion?

Reflection: Am I living in the truth of my means? Have I been in the reality of my existence? What measures should I consider to live in the abundance that I desire? Who has been placed on my path who can aid me to regain the balance that I lost?

Affirmation: I accept the clarity I have been afforded. I am open to the abundant gifts that the Universe has in store especially for me.

Prisoner / Prisionera
Reflect on the events that have led to incarceration
While awaiting release gather your spiritual resources and strengthen your soul
Freedom will always be attained at the end

Graciella sits in a darkened prison cell. A brightly colored parrot is perched next to her. A vivid sunrise is visible through the window's iron bars.

Incarcerations may be of the physical, emotional, or spiritual kind. Prisons are usually of our own making, although the sentence, *I was in the wrong place at the wrong time,* is often uttered in defense. We may fight against the notion that our own actions have resulted in our incarcerations. We may be held behind metal fences, gates with heavy locks suspended on thick chains, or leaden barriers to the outside world. Imprisonment might be a jail term for a crime or being held hostage in a relationship in which we feel stifled or even in fear for our lives. Our tears gush forward. Depression looms large. There is a feeling of powerlessness that pervades our being. Someone we love may be incarcerated and we are unable to easily gain access to these individuals.

Can we be honest with ourselves about the reasons we are in such a dismal plight? Were the actions we took so severe that we are locked away from a life of sunshine, delight, and freedom? We are encouraged to acknowledge our truths. Do we continually blame others for our dilemma? Was it the judge, the jury, or the decisions we made that have us wishing for another reality?

Seclusion affords us time to reflect on our circumstances. Whether we use the time to consider our situations is yet another decision with which we are faced. During our sequestered time, after we have determined the underlying reasons or excuses that we have erected, we can then seek the help that might have been within reach but were not ready to access. Courage and perseverance will be necessary as we work our way out of our entrapment, building new patterns of being.

Reflection: How have I participated in my state of confinement today? What actions have led me here and what actions may I take for release? Is there someone I trust to lend a guiding way out of these circumstances?

Affirmation: *I act toward freedom. I walk on the path of liberty.*

Rascal / El Travieso

Sly as a fox, crafty, and clever
Child-like in his ways
He may be an errand boy sent to glean information
Or he may simply reflect your actions in the world

    A young boy enjoys a hoop game as he walks down a cobble stone street. A little white dog loyally follows him. Outside of the boy's vision, a dark shadowy figure watches him. A fruit stand holds red and green fruit that are for sale. A green awning protects the produce from the strong sun.

    Graciella reminds us that there is always a rascal in our lives and sometimes that rascal is us. The energy of the rascal is pugnacious, fun-loving, and lives with no holds barred. You may find him or her in your immediate environment or it could be someone behind the scenes confounding all that you think you know. Think of the trickster who is the one who backs away saying, *I didn't mean any harm!* Why would they say this? Because they truly don't mean any harm to come your way.

    The rascal enjoys his deeds for today. He may be here to trick you, or he will get tricked himself. It's a toss-up. The rascal usually gets away with their clever acts that leave us shaking our heads. Do not give this individual more power than they deserve. There is no need to get in turmoil over something superficial. We tend to think of the trickster as one who is out to make a person seem the fool. Instead, think of that imp as one who brings fun and joy and a different understanding of ourselves. They may bring merriment to a place where life is stark and dull. It is a clever trick for some of us not to make a day of joy into one of sorrow. The idea that things aren't exactly as you think they should be may get in the way of your happiness. We are all works in progress.

Try not to succumb to a whim or let yourself down at the new information brought your way. Work with it; stealthily, craftily. Be the rascal. There's no need to have the rug pulled out from under your feet. If it happens, laugh heartily, and quickly release the resulting embarrassment or discomfort. Be forgiving. There is no one-upmanship if you move and progress steadily with light and love in your eyes. The Great Mother always stands behind you to support you.

Reflection: Why is it that the mischievous actions of others result in my losing my balance? Why do I give more power to annoyances than they deserve? Is it possible to join in and just enjoy myself?

Affirmation: *I take my toys out to play and open my circle! I enjoy my life!*

Romantic / Romántica

Wistful and hopeful
No promises have been made
Allow what is desired to happen naturally
Don't attempt to do the shifting

Graciella's dress is white, symbolic of purity and innocence. A flowering fruit bush symbolizes the work she has done for her growth. She appears to be leaving a cotillion or maybe a hall of mirrors and holds onto a sturdy handrail as she leaves.

Spirit whispers to us as a breeze. Romanticizing a want or a desire is key to creating a vision. Fall in love with it. Engaging in fantasy and imagination can be healthy and sane if the groundwork is also done for our dreams to come to fruition. Allow the seeds to grow into a fruit bearing tree. You have watered your seedlings and have made certain that the soil is rich in nutrients. The planting may not bear fruit this year or the next. It may take a while before you savor the fruits of your labor. Believe in your inner knowing that your vision will come true. Allow it to bloom naturally.

There are positive points to being a romantic. We are allowed to gaze without purpose and to move easily without a preconceived notion of what are to be our next steps. By being fanciful we emerge with ideas that we would never have encountered had we not allowed ourselves the gift of reverie. There is also the contrasting force of being purposeful with a plan to work toward. We set objectives and act, knowing that a goal will be achieved. We are rigorous with our process and accomplish what we never thought possible. Enjoy the balance.

The idea of romanticism is often looked at in an askance manner. When told we are romantics we may hear the underlying message that we are not serious about a particular course of action. The fine thing about having our heads in the sky is that many dreams are born there. These dreams can manifest if we take time to develop a plan. Begin by writing a note or saying a prayer. Send your dreams into the Universe. Have faith in your vision as you move forward on your path. Allow the beauty of your vision to expand and what you seek to come to you.

Reflection: What keeps me from believing in my dreams and creating my vision? Do I give myself the time I deserve to be one with my desires?

Affirmation: *I envision a creation manifested by the love nurtured in my being.*

Sobriety / Sobriedad

Surrendering to That Which Is unfurls a path
Explore with clarity and purpose
Maneuver the unpredictable terrain
With willingness and love

A hand is about to insert a key into a lock. There are green mountainous lands seen through the door's glass panes.

It is a great responsibility to live with a clear vision of the path that is before us. If we turn around, for a moment, we can observe the path that we have treaded on until today. The errors, the misjudgments, and the aftermath of our decisions are revealed to us.

While acknowledging faults we have made, we are given the opportunity to progress forward. We may be in fear of this walk as it is new to us. We may encounter unfamiliar faces on our journey so it will take courage to move forward. We may be determined to forge ahead, yet we miss those loved ones that have accompanied us on our old journey.

Take pause. Breathe deeply and exhale. As you continue your breathwork, envision for yourself what a life of clarity and purpose will mean for you. Is it one that you've hoped for? Or one that you've dreaded because you've gotten used to the old way of life that is one of darkness and isolation. Mobilizing into sober living, we shift the energies of our sacral chakras. Our understanding of our families, our lineage, our memories will change along with our movement. As we progress through levels of awareness, we decipher what has been our part in relationship to ourselves, our loved ones, and in the larger world.

There are many light beings on this planet who are willing to help as we move toward new paths. If we listen, we hear the offers and the promises of living in clarity. We take the hands of those who are willing to walk alongside us. We lift our faces to the higher energies of the Universe. Awareness can be subtle and sometimes blinding as we grow in new ways. We give thanks and then we become light beings and seers who reach our hands out to those who walk behind us, looking for the light on their own paths, and we share our experience.

Reflection: Am I ready to conspire with the Universe as it offers me clarity? Am I still comfortable walking on familiar paths that may not be for my higher purpose on this Earth? Must I give up all to accept a new way of being?

Affirmation: *My heart and mind are open to the gentle shifting of the old ways already known to me. I accept the new that is in alignment with my higher purpose.*

South / Sur

Raise your face to the sun
You are protected and guided
Trust that which Spirit shares with you
Know that all will be shown clearly in its time

With eyes closed, Graciella turns her face up to southern breeze. She is surrounded by trees and rocky formations are at her back.

The South is the direction that brings forward truth in simplicity. An innocence in knowing that what *is* can be trusted. Spiritually, this can be experienced more fully when we have a deep relationship with our Higher Power. We are not alone and while we may have a notion that something is amiss or that we are entering new territory, we have deep awareness we are being guided and protected.

How does one develop the ability to lean into the idea that one is cared for? There are prayer and meditation, processes that worked with slowly over time, evolve toward not only trusting in our Higher Power, but ourselves. When we engage in these practices, we are encouraged not to discount what we see and what we hear.

Allow for the possibility that negative thoughts or memories may come forward when working with the energy of the South. Remember that as we open our beings to the idea of trust, that those things that proved to be untrustworthy may peek through for their last hurrahs. We allow them to show themselves, but we need not be overcome and overwhelmed. They do not own us. We are not in relationship anymore. We may say hello and then a quick good-bye.

At times, our earlier incarnations may ask for our attention when we are working with the concept of trust. These parts of ourselves may have been challenged or harmed in the past. Today, we can be kind and gentle even if these parts present themselves as irritable or angry. We give them time to adjust to newness and all it brings. We sit our today selves with our yesterday selves. We encourage love and foster forgiveness. We tell these parts of ourselves that we are in a new day and we, together, will not repeat patterns that have injured us. Within ourselves, we evoke trust. We grow to trust in a Higher Power. We become aware that as we expand our visions of ourselves that we expand our visions of our Higher Powers. We are then held in our new right-sized, trustworthy, selves.

Reflection: Have I allowed myself to look deeply within and to know myself? Have I pointed to others or outside situations as the sources of my discomfort and lack of trust? Have I relied on a Higher Power of my own to enrich my perspectives and sense of trust in myself and the world?

Affirmation: *I am immersed in beauty, and I trust that I am being shown the way to goodness both within and without.*

Spiral / Espiral

Ascend the helix without trepidation
While this is a familiar situation
It is not a repeat performance
Utilize experience to your advantage

Colorful ribbons flow from a tambourine and intertwine, reminiscent of a helix, like the strands of a DNA molecule.

Everyone is encouraged to be aware of their place in their ancestral lineage. We easily acknowledge those who came before us, but have we considered those who have come after us? These are the ones that we have birthed, the ones we have raised, and the ones we have mentored. We each are afforded our own strands, although we join others at the tympanic membrane of the drums that beat to life rhythms.

Climbing the double helix of our existence we recognize that conditions are not repeat performances. While the situation and the sentiments may seem familiar, it is important to know that we are not where or who we were in the past. Listen to the stories of those who lived before us, honor them but also honor the shining filaments of our own lives. There are those of us who ignore our own strands while we tend to the elders and to the children. We must maintain our dynamic ecosystems, our bodies, ourselves, to aid in the survival of our lineage and our planet.

Individuals may feel burdened and saddened when circumstances seem as though they haven't changed. When one has done inner work there comes a change in one's attitude, in the ability to accept, and in the actions one has the fortitude to take. What our ancestors did helped us to be who we are today. They are our powers of example whether in a positive or negative sense. Our children learn by our examples, but we cannot expect them to be us. They have their own strands to weave.

Be at peace within, knowing that collectively we can lift veils of deception and remove familial maladies. We dismantle causes that are disruptive to the wholeness and regeneration of our lineages and that affect the greater well-being of our planet. We connect to others of our lineage and are not alone.

Reflection: As I reflect on my place on the strand of my lineage, I ask: How have I have cared for myself? How have I made myself available to those in my circle of love.

Affirmation: *I respond in the manner that my Earth Mother urges and act and speak in truth with an open heart and mind.*

Spring / Primavera

Spring enters with a flourish
The prospect of revitalization arrives
Feel the subtle energies of renewal and purpose
Love sweetly beckons

Pink cherry blossoms fill the air with hope, beauty, peace, and tranquility.

We experience an inner spark of new life that gives us permission to dream, to live, and to fully participate in our vision that is a blessing that only we can provide for ourselves. We are reminded that the seasons change as we do and we are ever invited to walk on their cyclical paths. Although our external environment may at times seem lackluster or not encouraging to our instinctual drives, we needn't worry about phases that may seem out of tune with the seasons or elements. We may be experiencing a burst of Spring within ourselves during the season of Autumn that is usually representative of a time of release. This burgeoning revitalization has its own catalyst, of which we may or not be aware.

Have you set a project aside and felt its call this morning? Have you a sense of urgency or quickening as to a creative action that has remained dormant until this moment? Embrace this newness with love and joy in your heart. A new life purpose may have just been revealed. Revel in it. Listen to the inner awakenings.

We are encouraged to reflect on whether we allow those who remain unconscious of the goodness of life to stifle our joys and the goodness that is ours to experience. We are living in a time of complexity and there may be people significant to you who do not hold your same values. We are advised not to allow negativity to crush our tender petals of growth. Acknowledge others' responses but refrain from dwelling in non-supportive messages. Take note without allowing what doesn't belong to you to encompass your life.

Walk within the rays of the sun. Say yes to all that you have envisioned. Wonderful things are coming. Continue to fulfill the promises you carried into this lifetime. Stand up for what you have worked for and that which you believe. Continue in your process with faith that what is yours will belong to you if that is the will of your Higher Power.

Reflection: Have I looked at today as it is, a day for living and for happiness? Have I embraced the spark I hold within me?

Affirmation: *I visualize the tender shoots of my growth becoming stronger and reaching up toward the light of the Universe.*

Star / Estrella

*Your thoughts and ideas are random and scattered
As impossible to grasp as a shooting star
Sift through the chaos and learn your life patterns
Discover the order of your Universe*

Graciella, dressed in white, leaves the estate. Her eyes are downcast. She holds a crystal point in her hands. Above her a shooting star traverses across the sky.

There are times that we are confused by the chaos in our lives. Major planetary influences, personal challenges, and the addressing of inequities touch our deeply instilled fears and, for many, bring personal dis-ease and dis-comfort. We are not sure where to turn or how to proceed. We believe that we are ill-prepared in making sense of what is happening or where to go for help. The darkness in our lives seems to permeate our existences and we are seemingly unaware of the illuminating points that guide us. We may be distraught and pray for a shepherding light.

When our thoughts are like random shooting stars that light the night sky, we are reminded that there is a pattern to what seems chaotic. There is always order amongst the stars. Graciella encourages us to be gentle with ourselves in the dark night that inks our souls. We are urged to take time for quiet, meditation, and stillness to clear our minds of the worries that come and result in nighttime ruminations. If you receive this message and you personally don't feel affected, you are encouraged to bring this message of hope to those you are in contact with in your life. Know that being still and embracing the glimmering light that our crystal beings accept from the night skies will afford us an increased sense of inner peace and understanding.

We are each stars in our constellations of many lives. While some of us may desire a light that is seen by all, remember that together all light shines brightly. The tiny lights seen emanating from fairy mounds are just as delightful as the lights experienced from the aurora borealis. Shine on, your light is unique and meant to illuminate in this world.

Reflection: Do I allow myself to speak the language of the stars and to channel their wisdom from all eternity?

Affirmation: *I am a child of the stars. The light that emanates from them guides me and creates the clarity that I so desire.*

Summer / Verano

The ease of summer days and nights
Replaces a usually hurried pace
Enjoy the simple and effortless movement
Others wish to emulate your tranquil manner

Magnificent bright blue and pink hydrangeas symbolize the beauty of the warm summer months.

Graciella whispers to us of a glorious day and suggests we allow the beauty to seep into our beings. Be one with that which brings pleasure to our senses, and that is in perfect alignment with our beings. There are times that our hurried ways, filled with a disorganized busyness and lack of clarity, bring to us a desire for the beloved days and evenings of summer. The easy ways of the summer can be experienced at any time of the year.

We sometimes look outside of ourselves and wish that we could be like others who appear to walk in ease and are unconcerned with the details that create harried lives such as ours. These are the times that we are encouraged to look within to find that place of peace within ourselves. We all have it, the ability to access it can be a feat, but it is an enchanting gift that changes our lives.

We need not lose our sense of calm and tranquility while engaged in difficult activities. We can still take time to enjoy the marvels that the Universe has provided for us. These wonders include the scents, the breezes, or the vivid colors that surround us. They may also be found while standing in line, waiting to see a doctor or to buy groceries. Waiting for the post office to open to receive a long-awaited letter can be another moment to cherish. During challenging times, we can still be appreciative and grateful for the beauty that is within us and that surrounds us.

Reflection: Do I wish to emulate others who seem to walk in ease? Have I taken time to access peace within myself? Have I accessed the depths of the possibilities within me for tranquility and peace?

Affirmation: *I am grateful for the beauty of my world, both inside my being and in the environment that I have chosen to inhabit.*

Sun / Sol

Caught in the sun's intensity
Unobscured by shadow in spots of burning darkness
Discern the rising heat
Determine whether protection is needed

Graciella pauses before the glaring sun while standing on the desert sands. She protects her eyes with one arm while guiding her camel with the other. Her beloved beast carries her provisions and knows well how to navigate harsh terrains.

We often desire veils or at least sunglasses to protect our eyes and our souls from some of the things we witness. We are reminded to moderate ourselves so as not to be scorched by the harshness in our world. We are advised to mediate the glare of the sun of our experience with the cool reflective light of the moon.

We often declare that we desire clarity and that we are open to being clear channels for the higher good of the world. We then protect ourselves when we observe what may be too difficult to bear. Our children, our relatives, or ourselves may have been or are still steeped in shadow and we'd rather pass over that clarity and focus on more distant issues. Being in the light and of the light can be challenging. We are asked to deal with truths that we'd rather not. We consider whether it is easier to live in darkness and denial because the awareness that accompanies the light is too frightening to endure.

Fear is a default mode for many. Rationalization is another. We often do need to protect ourselves, but we must know from what we truly need protection. We may be hiding from an expanse of knowledge that will add to our ability to thrive and to grow as beautiful sunflowers. What is that fear that takes you away from your growth in this lifetime? Extend your arms to the sun. Gather its light into your hands. Hold that light with love and then bring your loving hands to your third eye and then your heartspace. Let the sun's loving awareness of all absorb into your being. Once you have done this, breathe and give thanks.

Reflection: Am I shielding myself against clarity? How may I gently reflect light during these challenging times?

Affirmation: *I embrace the light of the sun that ignites the light of my being.*

Temptation / Tentación

*Desires and hungers are awakened
Passions are stirred and the fires within are tended
Freeing hidden dreams and fantasies
Pouring forth beauty and voraciousness for life*

Graciella is seductive as she dances in her fiery red dress. The masculine image seems to be going toward her with a glass of plum-hued wine at his side. There appears to be a mirror behind the woman.

Graciella reminds us that temptation has the connotation of many things, often negative. We all struggle staying away from things that may not be beneficial for us. Things that may bring us sorrow, regret, and lament. There are those of us who might do a bit better if we stayed away from that second ice cream cone, one glass of wine too many, or our next-door neighbor's spouse. Likewise, we may become tempted by things that seem as though they are out of reach to us but may be beneficial to us. We may have been steered away from certain things by our elders only to find that the fears they held were unfounded. The teachings may have been applicable during their times, but we must assess whether our desires are safe for us. These may be crucial items that we deny ourselves as we plan for our futures. We may not proceed with satisfying our desires because of our own fears that we may not be on the right road.

We are advised to look into the mirror and reflect on what we see. It may be that our visions are blinded by the depths of our craving. Or we may find that we are prime for a new enterprise. Life is an adventure to be explored. There are always new terrains to cover. We are encouraged to allow ourselves optimistic points of view of what we are tempted to engage in, and we may very well find that temptation is something that would broaden our horizons in life. If needed, we are encouraged to seek out the counsel of a sage that may help us discern whether this seeming temptation will be beneficial for us.

Reflection: What is the motivation behind my profound desire? Have I allowed myself to explore different paths in my life? Have I denied myself in partaking of the wonderful things that have been placed before me? Will I or someone else be harmed by engaging in this desire or might I find healthy joy?

Affirmation: *I am clear in my motivations and enjoy the fruits of this lifetime.*

Temptress / Sirena
A mere whisper of seduction allures and captivates
Show yourself subtly
Be certain of the target of your aim
The desired will ultimately succumb to your charms

Graciella whispers into the ear of a masculine figure. She wears simple jewelry and coins of gold. The red of her lips matches the hue of her blouse.

When I whispered, you listened. In this world of noise and distraction, we take the time to listen. One listens to the words of the temptress because the message resonates. The temptress seduces us with her enchanting ways. A smile, a song, or the way one tosses their curls captivates us. We are the ones who are responsible for how we experience the messenger and the message.

The temptress tantalizes with words and promises that are longed for. We are warned against the effects of the seven deadly sins: pride, lust, gluttony, greed, envy, wrath, and sloth. We are cautioned about the ingestion of excessive sugary sweets, reckless consumption of liqueurs, wallowing in self-pity, and comparing ourselves to our fellows. We may not purposely desire some of these things, yet we still experience a mad yearning. Oh, how we crave!

What if the ideas of love, faith, healing, or a profound belief in a Higher Power were whispered in our ears? What if the lovely whispers or songs of the temptress were invitations to good health, trust or forgiveness? What then? Would we be tempted to indulge?

Think about how you tempt others. How do you flirtatiously invite them into your lair? Go beyond the skin depth of beauty, as both the temptress and they who are tempted. Whisper the words of compassion, love, and beauty, and see what you may find. Experience a new level of love.

Reflection: What or who distracts me from my path of love and compassion? How do I share the message of unity and love in the world?

Affirmation: *I receive messages that are of my highest good and I share them for the highest good of all involved.*

Toreador / Matador

Circling, spiraling, ready for the kill
Stealth, magnetism, power
Planning to satisfy your audience's thirst for blood
Acknowledge your true motive

A toreador faces his audience, authoritatively waving a red cloth. His uniform is well decorated. Just like the toreador, the audience is ready for the bull to appear.

The toreador embodies stealth, cunning, and wit. He is integral with the staging and blood-thirsty event that for him is not merely sport, but what he believes is a means of survival. Graciella reminds us that while we prepare for action, we must be prepared for any scenario that may unfold before us. The target of your motive may not be what you think it is. It gives pause to witness someone using their shrewdness and agility to face something or someone who really has no say or understanding of the coming events of violence and carnage.

We often make decisions and take actions that may not be essential for our highest good, although we have our best interests in mind. A toreador puts themselves in danger for applause as they tease, taunt, injure, and ultimately, murder animals as a sport, done for the enjoyment of others. Being aroused by such violence requires us to face the actions we take that are for the adulation of others. There are tales of toreadors who have walked away from engaging in spectacle when they have come to a deeper understanding of love and compassion for self and then other. You may decide to alter your moves when you truly understand the motives that lie beneath your actions.

Reflection: What are my motives? To what lengths will I go for applause and to show my skill. Could my desire for fulfillment be satisfied in another way?

Affirmation: *I accept my true motives, aware that I have the power to change my actions.*

Traveler / Viajera

Uncertain which path to follow?
Follow your intuition
Move forward on your journey
Be open to what you encounter

Graciella travels by train, her eyes are closed as she is lulled by rhythmical movement. She holds her guitar. A small parcel lies on the seat next to her. A large suitcase is placed close to her on the floor of a cabin. Through the windows behind her, we see verdant grounds, clear blue waters, and matching skies.

Graciella sweetly urges us to travel on our paths with Divine intercession. There are times that we may not know which way to head as we meet crossroads, forks in the road, obstacles, and sometimes, glaring stop signs. Have faith in your intuition. Know that if you have taken time to know yourself and heed your inner warning signals and the go-aheads you've heard whispered to you that you are in good stead. Know that you are guided in decisions as you walk or ride or even run on your path! The pure bliss of sound decision-making comes with daily reflection, prayer, and meditation.

Graciella suggests you prepare for a day or even a season of traveling. Just when we think that we cannot take more newness in, yet another thing comes knocking at our doors. We are encouraged to allow our beings to surpass anything that we've known before. The old thinking patterns are no longer useful, and we need a total overhaul of what we believe we can accomplish. In meditation, we are positioned for all senses of limitation to disappear. Know that all things are possible. Graciella reminds us that although we may feel stagnant and as though time is not moving, it truly is just as we are.

Remember, that none of us travels the path of life alone, although we may frequently feel this way. A sense of loneliness comes from deep within. We travel individual paths and yet, we are joined with the other beings on this planet to not only survive, but to thrive and bloom.

Reflection: What moves me on my inner path? What drives me on my outer path? What are my desires? How am I holding myself back from pursuing my dreams? Can fantasy become reality? What is my magic? How can I experience a new me?

Affirmation: *I am not alone. I am guided in my life's journeys. I listen to my intuitions.*

Treachery / Traición

Blinded to your own reflection
Self-will binds
Allow awareness to surge through your being
Refrain from self-betrayal

A masculine figure hangs from a tree limb by his jacket under the night sky. His hands are tied and his hat floats underneath him in a small pond. The feminine aspect sits at the side of the pond gazing into the waters. Her head is covered, and she holds a crystal in her hand. The wagon is behind them on a dirt path but not directly poised for movement.

Graciella reminds us that at times we are our own worst betrayers. How have you spent your day? Or your weeks or months? Have you taken care of your personal needs? Only you know what you have been neglecting. We are souls who spend time gazing at our reflections in mirrors with no introspection at all. We are adept in avoiding honest appraisal of ourselves. It may be too painful to go in and see what we are made of. It is frequently much easier to do assessment of others. By taking someone else's inventory, we are liberated from facing our self-truths.

We may carry the sense that we have been betrayed by someone other than ourselves, but it may very well be a betrayal of our own making. We spend time with friends knowing that we leave our creative work on the back burner. We may have binge watched a television series aware that the wonderful meal we had in mind wouldn't get cooked. While these are actions that may be needed for relaxation or camaraderie, we are encouraged to become aware of time that is wasted in procrastination.

Explore ways that you have debted yourself or acted in treacherous ways against yourself. Frequently, when we explore the terrain within, we connect the pain and hurt we find with what others have done to us. It can be difficult for us to assess our own actions that may have injured us. As we ask ourselves what parts we've played in the misconstruction of our lives, we may need the listening ear of another. We may benefit by bookending our exploration with a cool drink of lemonade or a walk amongst some flowers. There is no rule that tells us that when we engage in the challenging work of looking within that we must do so harshly. Gentleness is key.

Reflection: Am I ready to look within and accept who I am and how that is reflected in the world? Do I blame others when things don't go well? Am I honest and open with myself?

Affirmation: *I am worth the time I spend in introspection. My inner terrain benefits from the gentle nurturing I bestow upon myself.*

Wagon / Carreta

The spirit is housed within one's body
Breathe. Take stock. Note.
Is your wagon frayed?
Determine what aspects need tending

While at first glance the wagon appears brightly colored and in good repair, we note it is in the process of being spruced up and repainted.

Graciella reminds us that the physical body we inhabit may be due for upkeep. We often hear that we are spirits within bodies that are our temples. Are you in a state of weariness and uncertain of why you feel as you do? We often trudge forward on the path we have chosen for ourselves. It may be time to assess whether we have neglected our bodies or if there is damage to our beings that we've been ignoring. Observe how you have treated not only your physical being, but the emotional, mental, and spiritual aspects of yourself. They are integral to each other. Each aspect that you provide healing, nurturing, and love to impacts all the parts of yourself. Listen to your being. It will tell you what you need. Be honest in the conversation that you hold within yourself.

Self-care is essential for us to be who we are meant to be. Graciella's simple reminder is that this may be a time for assessment, repair, and renovation. The wagon, whether it is our living environment or our physical bodies, symbolizes the need for constant maintenance.

Our needs may be as basic as a richer and deeper sleep or a need to increase our intake of pure crystalline water for the regulation of our systems. Because our energy fields extend all around us, we are encouraged to take a moment to assess our environmental aspects as well. What is in your intimate or remote environment that needs a bit of nurturing? What might need a hug, sprucing up, or a dose of love? What might need a scrubbing, a painting, or a breath? Reflect and the need will be shown to you. It need not be a massive renovation or redoing. It may be the simple act of moving a couple of sweaters to the sweater drawer. A small action leads to illuminating transformations.

Reflection: What in myself or my environment needs nurturing? Do I need a hug or does my child? Do the windows need to be washed to allow the sunlight to radiate throughout my home? Or is it my soul that needs tending?

Affirmation: *I listen to my body and my soul and nurture myself toward healing. I assess my environment and focus on one action I can take toward wholeness and affirmed life.*

Water / Agua

*Surrender to the waters of the Great Feminine
Submerge yourself in a river or ocean
Play in Her mists, ice, snows, or the gentlest of warm rains
Her love heals*

Children sprinkle water as they play with a hose. They are enclosed in a front yard that is surrounded by a fence.

Water is vapor, liquid, ice, and snow. It comprises streams, oceans, rains, and salty tears. Water is sacred and used in many religious ceremonies and initiations. It is our hope and salvation. We are born from our mother's waters and are cradled in them before our births. We drink water for hydration and for survival. We play in fountain sprays. We often cry on rainy days. We sprinkle our lawns with water to ensure their growth.

Graciella encourages us to increase our awareness of our waters and to welcome water as a soothing element in our lives. Water is healing. Will the tears that roll down our cheeks heal our hearts full of anguish, fear, anxiety, or pain? Will dipping our toes in the ocean clear unwanted energies? Will taking a long walk in the rain provide the soothing we so desire and deserve? Is a lavender bath the tool for allaying anxiety today?

We are encouraged to reflect on how we may protect and love water. There are many programs that have been created to save our planet's waters. If one of these resonates with you, participate in it as a goodly project for the Earth's survival.

Take a bowl of your choice and fill it with clear water. Gaze softly into the water and watch as images and sounds emerge. Be patient with the process. It may take several times of doing this before you clearly discern pictures or patterns. Journal your experiences. Allow yourself the time and space needed in this endeavor.

Reflection: Have I created opportunities to experience a relationship with water?

Affirmation: *Water, I thank you for washing away what is no longer useful to me. Clear streams of love and health refresh me anew! Divine Feminine, I embrace You!*

West / Oeste

*The majesty of the West calls to you
The desires of your soul whisper softly
Spirit connects your inner and outer worlds
Reflect and your service will be revealed*

A majestic rock emerges from the depths of our Mother's ocean waters.

Graciella whispers to us about the mysteries of the west. The west is the place for deep reflection, for healing, for profound connection to the Mother's energies of love, depth, and sacred glory. While the west tells the histories of conquest and division, it also tells of survival and thriving amongst peoples who were plucked from their humanities in every sense.

The simple message of the west is to look within. Explore the terrain within you that is infinite in possibility and abundance. The harm of others is diminished when we connect with the compassionate realms within ourselves. When we become aware of who we are, how we respond, and our purposes in life in a manner of love and kindness, we are less likely to trample upon others. By honoring and valuing ourselves as individuals in the web of connectedness and love we are offered the opportunity to view and honor life from a higher perspective.

Reflection: How do I ground myself within the love of the Great Mother? What does my Higher Power provide me with for my inner sanctity? Am I open to the grandness of Her gifts?

Affirmation: *I am protected by the magnificence of the Great Mother Goddess and all Her glory. I walk this Earth in emulation of Her beautiful ways.*

Wind / Viento

The winds clarify your thoughts
Turbulent as a hurricane
Gentle as a baby's breath
Embrace the transformation

Graciella plays barefoot with her dog on green grass. The wind whips her hair about her face. The hem of the red cape flaps in the wind.

The wind is at times silent in its gentle persuasions and at other times speaks to us in gusts. The power of the winds stuns with its incisive nature. Have you ever seen the effects of a hurricane? A half dwelling may topple, and the second half stands straight and tall as though not even a breeze has been in the vicinity.

As children we learn that seasonal winds scatter seeds that will later become fruit bearing trees. We contemplate the seeming randomness of Earth's means of growth and development. This is certainly not how farmers grow their crops, methodically preparing the grounds, sowing the seeds, weeding, watering, and fertilizing. We are amazed at how something that appears to be so happenstance, successfully takes root. It is a wonder of nature.

We listen to whistling winds and branches that scrape against our windows. We hear words spoken aloud meant for us and sometimes those that are not. These words affect us in a great many ways. We carefully listen in quiet meditation. At times we hear nothing, at others, we allow the sounds to be absorbed by our beings. The sound carried by the air may take the form of a child's laughter, an owl hooting in the night, or the memory of a verbal caress from a loved one. We are at peace, knowing these sounds are nurturing, bringing us to states of bliss.

At times, we hear messages without having discerned actual voices, merely the waves of sound at a frequency that are above the register that we usually hear. We know intuitively that what we have heard is true and real for us and we act based on these gentle winds of knowledge that have made their way into our consciousness. Allow yourself in a session of automatic writing to revel in the wisdom of the air you breathe, the winds that create the flickering of a candle that is set in a closed room. Believe in the power and truth of the winds.

Reflection: Do I listen to the messages that the winds bring to me? Do I share the wisdom that seems to have come so easily through the graceful dance of air?

Affirmation: *I follow the course directed to me by the winds. I embrace the transformations for which I have prepared.*

Winter / Invierno

Barren trees are covered in blankets of white snow
Be soothed by the respite
Knowing that these dormant times will culminate
In accordance with Mother Nature's laws

A light falling snow touches tree branches that at first glance appear barren. Berries adorn the tips of some of the limbs.

The peaceful winter season brings serenity and a sense of calm. It brings a time of rest and an opportunity of gathering to oneself. The season is known for its joys in quiet ways or is sometimes raucous with sleighs traversing down snowy slopes. The time is usually appreciated for its tranquility.

While the season brings holidays that people of different faiths celebrate, there comes the time for withdrawal that brings balance to our lives. Some of us are not willing to indulge in these times. We are keen for continued merriment without pause for regeneration. We are encouraged to follow the seasons and to be in the rhythms of nature.

Under the ice-laden coverings of the earth, we are reminded that in still repose lies the medium for fruitful growth. One of the wisdoms of Mother Earth is that She is careful to keep hidden what is not ready to be revealed. She encourages us to be as nature and to take our time with our endeavors. A splashy display of spring flowers is being carefully cultivated by the earth, the winds, and the rains. The time afforded for the growth and maturation of our trees, shrubs, and flowering plants should be considered when we plan our projects and our endeavors. We, as natural children of the Mother, are urged to remember the bounty that She brings to our existences.

Sit in stillness as you reflect on this card. Allow your thoughts to come naturally and be in awe of the revelations that come to you. We are a manifestation of life and love, and we are urged to revel in the beauty of ourselves and the world around us.

Reflection: Do I allow myself to enjoy the stillness of the winter season? In what ways can I allow myself to be?

Affirmation: *My heart beats in rhythm with the Mother's seasons and I rejoice in them.*

Wisdom / Sabiduria

*Learning the way
Comes with the passage of time
Wisdom and knowledge cannot be bought
But must be earned*

An elder enjoys her pipe on the porch of her modest home. She appears to be in thought or maybe reading the smoke curling from the pipe. The tree near the house holds secrets within the branches. By listening closely one can hear the stories of dreams and lives of the generations of those who have lived in that house.

Honor the ways of the elders. They are the bearers of time-worn ways that, although still viable and that may lead to a thriving life, are often forsaken in favor of the new. We seek out wisdom from those who we trust. While many of us speak about the wonders of our experiences with our elders and share of the love we have for them, there are those of us who may not have been so fortunate. We may not know who our elders are or there are elders' behaviors that we do not want to emulate. We may have been given the message that it would be distasteful or dishonorable if we share our truths of hardships with our elders. Our truths are our truths.

The wisdom of elders may be available to us from those who are not blood relatives but who are willing to share with us from their own experience, strength, and hope.

Searching for someone who has garnered years of knowledge and experience with full compassion is a laudable task. There are times that the teachers seem busy, don't hear what we ask, or are out of reach of our needs. Asking these learned people for their time and their wisdom is one of the challenging tasks in walking the way of enlightenment. Be at peace that you will find those teachers that you seek. Answers will appear when the Universe decrees.

At some point in our lives, we become the elders. We are gently reminded that we too can only give what we have accumulated in our experience. There are those of us who take on more than we can handle, whether it be in teaching or providing words to others that we are ill-prepared to speak. As always, go within and ask for humility to be truthful in what has been experienced, what is true knowledge, and discern whether we speak through ego.

Reflection: How will I respond today to the situations that cross my path with the knowledge and wisdom I have gathered over the years? Am I ready for revelation in my quest for wisdom?

Affirmation: *With open arms, I welcome the light beings who have come to provide me with the knowledge and wisdom that I seek.*

Writer / Escritora

Your words flow like a waterfall
Filled with the riches of the oceans and rivers
Colorful fish swim amongst the coral
Others experience them and are delighted

A blank page is set in an old-fashioned typewriter awaiting the message that is to be written. Next to the typewriter is the golden bracelet of friendship, pink roses in full bloom, and golden fishes swimming in the clearest of waters. These are symbols of love, beauty, and life.

Words are the most powerful tools and weapons we have on this planet. They are our sharpest knives and in contrast can be sweet— like pollen to bees. Conveying our messages with compassion takes forethought and planning. Our thoughts are channeled onto the empty page or open person and can be constructive or destructive. It is wise to reflect on the immense power of communication that one yields and each of us is urged to act accordingly. We can be harmed and divided with carelessly spoken words. We can mend rifts when we choose wisely and intentionally.

Many individuals don't pause before sharing their senses of feeling unjust, their misconceptions, or feeling of a lack of value they are experiencing. When feeling hurt one may be tempted to share messages of harm toward others. Angry people may have a desire to incite anger in others. Graciella advises us to listen to our thoughts before they manifest into words. We are encouraged to be aware of the words we choose to use and the reasons for using them.

Words tell stories, whether of a true narrative or a tale received from the downloads of the Universe or the muse who whispers in our ears. The ideas we develop into these tales may seem a gift to some and a curse to others. We may be ambivalent about sharing words, yet they are designed to be shared with another. Kindness is always key. We have the power to accept or dismiss the words we are being told. Listen with discernment. We are responsible for the intended messages we share on paper, electronically, and via the microphones that we are privileged to use.

Reflection: Are my communications clear and compassionate? Will my words manifest toward healing today?

Affirmation: *I convey the messages of love and goodness needed in this world.*

Spreads

Graciella's oracle will respond to those who seek knowledge about themselves or situations that pertain to themselves. Graciella encourages you to spend time with the cards to familiarize yourself with how the oracle responds to you. Once you have developed a relationship with the oracle, reading for others becomes a spiritual service. Please obtain permission prior to doing a reading for someone as this is a private enterprise. The querent may request a reading for a lover, a child, or a friend. Ask permission from that person before engaging in that activity. Instead, you may pose your questions on the situation in relation to the querent.

Graciella suggests setting up a daily exercise that you can easily accomplish. There is no one right way to meditate. For some sitting quietly for a few moments is effective. Others may prefer more ritualized ways of meditation with the use of candles, obsidian mirrors, or using other techniques in which you may have been trained.

When preparing to consult the oracle, I usually burn sage in a small abalone shell and use a feather to smudge myself, the cards, and the room in which I am sitting. I may burn cedar in the shell or small bowl or light a cedar stick to invite helpful energies into the room. I open a window for the release of various energies that must go on their way.

I take a few cleansing breaths and sit comfortably, allowing my chest and abdomen to expand with a few subsequent deeper breaths. I imagine myself as a conduit for Universal luminous light that channels through me starting at my crown chakra through my body and out through the energy centers of my feet. The light becomes roots that connect me under the Earth and grounds me, tethering me to The Great Mother.

Having centered and grounded, I place the cards in front of me on an uncluttered flat surface. I center myself and then shuffle the cards at least three times. I place them in front of me face down, spread open like a fan and focus on Graciella's image in my mind's eye. I either ask her a specific question or a more general question of what I should focus on throughout the day or in a chosen situation. I often keep my eyes closed and let my fingers feel for the card that wants to be picked from the deck. Once pulled, I turn the card over and consider the concept offered and how it may pertain to my current life situation or question. Then I write down my impressions and visualizations in a journal that I use solely for this purpose. I gather the other cards in a pile and place the concept card face up on the pile. At the end of the day, I look at the card again and consider how the concept has manifested itself to me during the day.

If my time is limited, I will do a quick read simply by shuffling, concentrating on Graciella's image, asking my question, and pulling a card from the oracle deck. When seeking responses from the oracle, be open to what your senses perceive. A phone ring, a knock on the door, a dog's sudden bark in otherwise quiet surroundings, or the aroma of baking muffins may be part of the message you receive.

Sample layout designs:

The following are several possible suggestions for drawing cards. No reading is fixed. They are mutable and therefore there is no need for you to become stuck as to the glory or devastation that you may perceive is conveyed from a particular card. Understandings of the past can be altered by a differing outlook or by the receipt of new information after an initial experience of a situation. Awareness of the impermanence of life is an ingredient for healing. If I pull a reverse card from the deck, I merely turn it right side up. You, of course, may choose to review a reverse card as a challenge.

One Card Layout

The Now

One card is pulled from the deck for clarity on a particular situation, insight into your deeper motives or possibilities in relationships in the present. The one card can also be used if you don't have a specific question but would like to increase your general awareness of the meaning of the card. I continue to use this one daily as the cards are dynamic and give ever-changing messages always providing further illumination.

Three Card Layout 1

1. Past   2. Present   3. Future

This spread provides information on the past, present, and future possibilities of an issue or situation. Prepare for a reading as previously described and then pull three separate cards, placing them individually side by side, face down.

When readying to pull the card regarding *past* influences, be certain to focus *specifically* on the past. For this card your goal is to obtain information on what has already transpired. While we needn't stare at the past too long, it can reveal a great deal about the background story as to how we arrived at the place we find ourselves in today. This card represents the recent past or the historical influence of today. Turn the far-left card first for a perspective on the past and how it relates to your question.

The middle card, *present*, is then turned over and placed next to the first card. This card provides information on today in relation to the situation or question posed. While you may think you know what is happening currently, there are always behind-the-scenes actions that you may not be privy to in the situation. It may be that patience is needed, you may receive information that you had not thought of prior to this moment. As always, be open.

The third card provides information on *future* possibilities available during the time the card is turned over. Again, remember that the future is mutable and not fixed. Be aware that you may sit with the card over a period of time to allow yourself to fully absorb the information. I often allow the cards to remain where I've placed them and return to them later in the day with a fresh perspective.

Three Card Layout II

1. Head   2. Heart   3. Will

For this three-card spread, the cards are placed in a vertical layout. The top card represents the *head* or your knowledge or ideas about the situation being explored. The middle card represents the *heart* or what your feelings and emotions are regarding the topic. The bottom card represents your *will* or desires in the question you have posed to the oracle.

Four Card Layout I

1. Head   2. Heart   3. Will   4. Higher Power

In this spread, we set the cards as in the Three Card Layout II, however, we pull another card in the deck and place it to the right of the vertical set up. This fourth card represents what our own designated Higher Power may desire for us. By weighing our thoughts, feelings, and desires with that of Something Greater than Ourselves, we are able to walk on a path that is of our Highest Good.

Four card Layout II

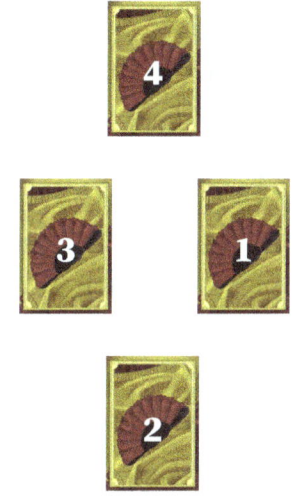

1. East   2. South   3. West   4. North

The cards are placed in the directions that pertain to each card, respectively. I suggest having a small compass in hand. While you may know your directions based on your living space, you may be reading at other locations. When involving the four directions, consider what you know about that direction and have those thoughts or images as background to each card you pull relating to the question. Pulling cards for each direction is a layered process. The querent is requesting information on a topic and the direction is the basis for that answer.

The *East* will illuminate us with information. Just as in the morning light, we are shown detailed specifics in bright clarity. We must want to have the knowledge and desire clarity when we ask questions. All the advice goes nowhere if we are hesitant in accepting enlightenment in our thought processes.

The *South* symbolizes trust. Spirit or Universe, however you deem That Which is Greater than yourself, knows what it takes for you to move through your existence, what strengthens, and what may be alarming or frightening for you. Spirit protects and provides the tools for you to course through life. With deep faith and belief, you will have the ability to trust in what manifests for you.

The *West* reflects our internal lives. It signifies our healing ways, our Medicine, the Sacred gifts that we each have. The West speaks to us about our motives, our expectations, and our assumptions. We discern whether our inner beliefs reflect who we are today or need reevaluation.

The *North* is the home of our ancestors who have passed on from the physical realm. They come to impart the wisdom ways to us who remain on this earth if we allow them to communicate with us. The North reminds us to reconnect with the simpler ways of life, walking the paths of wisdom who have walked on this earth before us.

About the Author

Theresa Varela is the award-winning author of the Daisy Muñiz Cozy Mystery Series and the Graciella la Gitana Oracle Deck. Her creative writings are woven with strands of mystery and psychology with a psychic twist. They encompass the experiences of Latinx and LGBTQ+ people in the urban landscape. Theresa holds a PhD from New York University and has worked in mental health for many years in New York City. She is a board member of the SistersInCrime, New York Tri-State Chapter, and member of Crime Writers of Color, Queer Crime Writers and Mystery Writers of America. Her website is www.theresavarela.com. She can be found on social media at IG: @TheresaVarelaAuthor, Bluesky: @theresavarela.bsky.social and Facebook: @theresavarela

www.ingramcontent.com/pod-product-compliance
Lightning Source LLC
Chambersburg PA
CBHW050611100526
44585CB00034B/1258